Antique Silver
and
Silver Collecting

Antique Silver
and
Silver

John Culme
John G Strang

Hamlyn
London · New York · Sydney · Toronto

Collecting

To Jane Fleur

Published by
The Hamlyn Publishing Group Limited
London · New York · Sydney · Toronto
Hamlyn House, Feltham, Middlesex, England

© Copyright The Hamlyn Publishing Group Limited 1973

ISBN 0 600 38023 8

Phototypeset and printed in England by
Sir Joseph Causton & Sons Limited

1 *half-title page* A George III tankard.
Samuel Whitford senior. London, 1815.
2 *title pages* A George III silver-gilt five-light
candelabrum. Benjamin Smith senior.
London, 1815. A George III coffee pot.
Jonathan Swift. London, 1761.
3 *right* Plate 6 (detail) from Knight's book of
Vases and Ornaments, etc., 1833, showing a
design for a two-handled cup and cover
[see also **4**].

Contents

Preface

Collecting silver judiciously is, up to a point, an exercise in taste. Sometimes an item is easily identifiable by its hallmark and its appearance. These alone tell the collector little about its relative worth, its stylistic parentage or its social background. It may be unique, or it may be commonplace though attractive enough.

The discriminating collector, therefore, requires a knowledge of styles. He has to be able to say whether it is a good or bad example of its kind. He has to be able to distinguish the original from possible reproductions. In this a knowledge of methods of production is useful. Naturally an ability to identify the silversmith or firm who made it is a great asset. A history of individual makers and manufacturers can help the collector to judge the craft or artistic merit of the article.

Rather than give ready-made scales of value or current market trends, which would be out of date before the book could reach print, we have tried to give the reader a basic knowledge of those lasting aspects of silver which are not the product of commercial instability but relate directly to the silver object itself. They are:

The stylistic development of silver
Methods of production
The social and historical background
The value of silver as art or craft

Knowledge of these gives us the ability to make an objective appraisal of any piece of silver as a genuine antique whose worth is assured.

We have placed particular emphasis on the 19th century, a period which has been neglected, but is now growing fast in importance in the salerooms. The continuity of silver production has been stressed— dates like 1700, or 1830 or 1851 are often arbitrary and unhelpful.

Possibly the only time when continuity is broken occurs in the middle of the 17th century. At that time much silver was melted down and sold as bullion to help Charles I in his expensive struggle against Parliament. When in 1660 silver was again in demand fashions had changed, and new designs were needed. Furthermore, silver from before 1660 is both rare and costly, and this book for collectors therefore begins at this date.

The silver of the last chapter shows the rise of design consciousness as a modern phenomenon. In each period, however, we have described the salient features which allow the collector to enjoy placing his antique in its proper perspective.

The maker's marks of numerous English silversmiths have been chosen as a guide to supplement the text of this book. Of necessity these are only a representative group illustrating their general design throughout the period covered, and each is accompanied by an approximate date. These marks, however, are frequently not the only examples associated with any one silversmith or manufacturer, nor do they apply to the whole working life of that individual or company. The majority of the English makers mentioned are London ones, so it may be assumed that a maker is London-based if no other location is given.

Throughout the book close attention has been paid to the importance of individual silversmiths and manufacturing firms and their relative merits, in order to give the collector a firm basis for discrimination: and that, after all, is the surest basis of wise investment. Dates are often given, for they are invaluable in any historical perspective, and an understanding of antiques is primarily an understanding of history itself, in our case, the history of silver. Our aim has been to impart the knowledge which will allow a collector to rely more confidently on his *own* judgement.

John Culme
John G. Strang

4 Plate 8 from Knight's book of *Vases and Ornaments, etc.*, 1833, showing suggestions for a six-light centrepiece, together with other small decorative details [see also **3**].

A. Wright Del.

T. Dick Sc.

Published by F. Knight, 12, Brooke Street Holborn and T. Griffiths, 3, Wellington Street Strand.

Introduction

Silver is not only useful: it is beautiful. For more than three thousand years men have enshrined the wisdom of empires and religions in silver. From silver diadems to chalices, from coin to teaspoons, it has symbolised man's search for identity and reassurance. To fashion, own or even use the plainest cup has for many been the sign not primarily of wealth, but of dignity.

The discerning collector who takes time to think about the most common item of silver with some knowledge of its context will find that the beauty or the oddness of the piece is a window into the inner world of man's culture. An engraved snuffbox may not have the symphonic significance of the Sutton Hoo Treasure, or a silver-backed hairbrush the dark mystery of a finely wrought reliquary for saintly bones: nevertheless they introduce us to the anecdotal flavour of history. Frivolity, romance, pomposity and even mystic visions have been melted into ingots, hammered, punched, chiselled, cut, moulded and mass-produced in a thousand ways. In short, silver involves people, and who people are. It lets us gossip a little, laugh a little, and sometimes take deeper stock of our values.

Anyone, therefore, who collects silver for its investment value alone misses much. To feel a piece of Queen Anne silver, for example, with its cool blue lustre, to study the proportions thoughtfully and to consider its details and artistry elevates us above the mischief of finance and the snobbery of taste. In its finest forms silver almost lives. Like velvet, or polished wood, it invites touch, sight and thought. It is this magic that makes silver rare.

For the average person, however, silver means the 'good spoons' and Grannie's teapot, and that, more than likely, will be electroplate. If silver it be, then the chances are that it is Victorian and hardly unique, though as we shall see, Victorian silver has a dignity of its own.

On the other hand, the tables of the maisonettes in Chelsea or the penthouses in New York may be adorned with shiny new silver. Apart from a few expensive craft pieces, these tend not to reflect the highest virtue of either the metal or the silversmith. Moreover it may cost more than antique silver. Sense and sensibility as much as the instinct of the collector or the connoisseur make it worthwhile to look around for much of the admirable old silver that is available and useable. To help any person to choose with understanding and discrimination is the simple aim of this book. It is more important that those who have, or would like to have, antique silver should learn to enjoy the 'Queen of Metals'.

5 A William IV large salver, 'enchased . . . with Dianthus flowers'. Edward Barnard & Sons for Robert Lowe, silversmith of Preston. London, 1830. George Eliot, in *Adam Bede* (1859), describes how it might have been used : '. . . but on this cloth there is a massive silver waiter with a decanter of water on it, of the same pattern as two larger ones that are propped up on the sideboard with a coat of arms conspicuous in their centre.'

Late Stuart Silver

In 1660 Charles II arrived in London as a constitutional monarch whose revenue came from Parliament. The Parliament which met in 1661, however, and lasted for seventeen years was intensely loyalist and Anglican, and was known as the 'Cavalier' Parliament. Silver, like politics, also became 'Cavalier'.

The silver which had been melted down during the Civil War had to be replaced, and the demand was for silver which celebrated the return of the beheaded Charles's son. With few exceptions, the silver of Cromwell's Commonwealth had been unsophisticated and scarce, consisting mostly of drinking vessels, bowls and spoons. The new, however, returned to the world of decoration and imagination. Heavily chased or embossed work became more fashionable, and Renaissance motifs were reworked. (For explanations of 'chasing' and other technicalities, the reader should consult the Glossary on page 90.)

There was one revolution, however, which could not be undone, namely the Puritan one, which to this day has influenced English outlook and values. Finely worked silver symbolised the return to royal and civil order. It also marked the dominance of the parliamentary-minded merchant class. These merchants in a real sense understood their worldly success as a mark of God's grace. For them silver plate expressed both the success and the grace. Silver, as it were, enshrined the principles of good economics, ecclesiastical propriety, Christian prosperity and individual success.

Expensive wars, civil and European, as well as the decline of Spain, had caused inflation. Generally there was a shortage of bullion. Nevertheless, the demand for silver increased, for in any period of instability people invest their money in non-devaluable goods. Silver was ideal. In order to find money, plate was melted down. Conversely, if plate was in demand coinage had to be converted. Goldsmiths and silversmiths did so without hesitation. This was not difficult, for the standard of both was required by law to be the same, as it had since Henry II's day. Coin-clipping, of course, was an attempt to have both coin and plate.

This depletion of the coinage had to be checked. Consequently in 1695 an Act of Parliament was passed forbidding publicans to use silver except for spoons. Until then it had become common practice in taverns to use silver tankards, mugs and basins. Today bars lose thousands of glass mugs each year. How much more tempting must silver have been. Indeed, robberies with violence were common, as the Grand Jury of Middlesex pointed out in 1695. This Act had little effect. So in 1697 an Act was passed raising the purity of silver from the Sterling standard (925 parts per thousand) to the Britannia (958·3 parts per thousand). In order that the new standard could be distinguished, the Act ordered that the maker's mark

'. . . be expressed by the first letter of his surname, the marks of the mystery or craft of the Goldsmiths, which, instead of the Leopard's Head and the Lion, shall for this plate be the figure of a woman, commonly called *Britannia* and the figure of a *lion's head erased . . .*'

Such legislation tells us that throughout this period demand was greater than supply. Demand is the barometer both of a nation's sense of values and of her prosperity. Moreover, the scarcity of bullion perhaps explains why much 17th-century plate is of a relatively thin gauge.

Charles II had spent part of his exile in Holland. The Dutch were a great mercantile nation, and the very reasons that made Holland Britain's rival meant that the merchants of Antwerp and Amsterdam had much in common with the London traders. A common hatred of Spain, a Protestant heritage and a Puritan range of values meant that the domestic magnificence of Dutch silver and designs had a ready acceptance in Restoration London. Late Elizabethan decoration had involved fruit, flowers and leafage, and the Dutch styles recaptured the richness of this pre-war silver. The art of embossing in high relief (repoussé) in the Dutch manner was further 7 encouraged. This produced decoration which served the double purpose of ornamentation and reinforcement. Metal strips were sometimes applied inside the piece to cover puncturing. Romantic monsters appear amidst the luxuriant foliage. Dutch styles also favoured elongated lobes, which were employed in a restrained manner, marking the direct influence of the Utrecht masters Adam and Christian van Vianen. Indeed, the latter had worked for Charles I from about 1637 to 1640. The architectural mood of art strongly emphasised form, while acanthus leaves, repoussé masks, amorini, flowers, fruit, animals and cast caryatid handles were highly reminiscent of designs for Dutch marquetry-work. Such decoration was disciplined. By the 1680s, however, as the decoration on late Restoration silver shows, Dutch influence was on the decline. Paradoxically by the time William, Prince of Orange, arrived in London in 1689, new styles from France were in the ascendant, and English silver was benefiting from the domestic policies of Louis XIV.

10

7 A Charles II salver with repoussé decoration. Maker's mark: H. London, 1663.

8 A James II porringer with flat-chased Chinoiserie decoration. Maker's mark: A.H., star above, crescent below. London, 1685.

France had emerged from the Thirty Years War as the strongest, most prestigious and brilliant European state. It was in the France of the Sun King that Charles II had also spent part of his exile. If the English court lived on French food, it also adopted French clothes and developed a taste for French architecture and furnishings. Silver was no exception.

The style of Versailles and the Louvre was that of the Baroque, largely the product of Italian designers like Bernini. By 1665 men of the genius of Wren were being influenced by it. The new saloons at Windsor reflected this taste, while the painted ceilings of Verio, a Neapolitan, teem with allegorical figures which swarm above the richly carved cornices of Grinling Gibbons (1648–1720). Amidst the leaves and fruit animals appear, yet the asymmetrical profusion, detailed and almost three-dimensional, preserves a subtle balance of architectural form. It was thought that this reflected the work of antiquity.

The silver of the period which began after about 1680 can be understood in terms of the principles at work in this new, essentially architectonic style.

The structural form of the Baroque basically contains a whole range of movement which in turn reduces the impression of formality. It creates the illusion of vitality through an emphasis on rounded shapes and shadows. The form and texture of the piece control the light in which we see it. In turn it is this light that controls the balance and the harmony of the work. Light dissolves contours and creates new spatial relations between the constituent parts. These produce the clarity of an harmonic composition. The decorative details are used with this in mind. At Versailles Lebrun uses antique motifs to create a balance between vitality and order.

English silverwork of the late 17th century stands in this tradition. Decoration and the reordering of form by a skilful allocation of light produces, not the emotion of a Bernini sculpture, but a rich harmony. Restraint is the end product.

By 1685, as France moved towards the ideal of a single Catholic religion and Louis XIV revoked the Edict of Nantes, so 200,000 French Protestants were expelled. Among these were some of the most gifted artisans of the day. From the early 1670s many had come to England. Though their influence must not be overstated, Huguenot silversmiths, notably Pierre Harache senior, a native of Rouen, and David Willaume senior (died before 1728), who had come from Metz, raised the standard of silverwork in England. They, too, stood in the Reformed tradition. Ornamentation was subordinated to the form of the piece, a tendency that was later to find its classical expression in the clarity of Queen Anne silver. Simplicity and proportion are of the utmost concern, while gadroon borders, flutes and ropework edges give a sense of containment and balance.

7

8

9
10

9 Pierre Harache senior, working from about 1675, died 1700.

10 David Willaume senior, came to England from France in 1686, died before 1728.

Decoration, still concerned with the 'geometry of light', used classical ornament like acanthus leaves in a way that brilliantly redefined the meaning of the word 'taste'. It is the influence of these French silversmiths, many of whom were of provincial origin, that marks the transition to the fine silver of Anne's England.

In 1692 the metalrolling machine appeared. While it was 1728 before John Cook improved it, silver could now be rolled from ingots. Time spent on hammering-up a piece was cut. Prices fell, an even larger market was created, and the type of decoration known as cutcard 22 work was further encouraged. Thin pieces of silver, usually in leaf or strapwork patterns, were cut and applied like silhouettes to the body of the piece. On cups it was used as a calyx between the foot and the body, giving the appearance of support and lightness. Often it was used to embellish the joints of handles or spouts.

The application of cut metal in this way needed great skill since it was intended to be an integral part of the work, rather than an irrelevant addition. All traces of solder had to be wiped away, leaving clean crisp borders, as though the piece grew from its natural support, like petals from a bud. French silversmiths made use of husk motifs in much the same way. The fashion continued from about 1670 to 1715.

Craftsmen also gave careful treatment to handles, finials and all sorts of decorative details. Handles, especially on popular items like porringers, were usually cast in the form of caryatids springing from leafage. On flagons in particular handles preserve the plain scroll or loop designs. Nevertheless, not all good things were imported. The old English custom of decorating the barrels of items such as tankards, beakers and tumbler-cups with bands or areas of matting was still continued. Added to this the pounced or engraved initials, other trailing decoration and punched-work, all issuing from borders of embossed flutes, were popular and attractive.

A silver warmingpan sounds slightly unlikely, but from 1660 onwards there was hardly anything that could not be made from the metal. Unlike the Duchess of Portsmouth (1649–1734), not everybody had tables and fireplaces made of silver. But napkinhooks, salt cellars, two-handled cups and porringers were made in significant numbers, together with a chorus of inkwells, toilet-services, spiceboxes, ewers, tankards, beakers, tumblers and spoons, as well as the newly fashionable forks. In this, England followed France. Initially, one took one's own cutlery to a meal, and the three-pronged forks with broad trefid handles and similar spoons, along with steel-bladed knives, make up exquisite portable sets. Often in shark-skin cases, these came with spiceboxes and oval beakers engraved with exotic birds and leafage.

Charles II's court had some exotic touches. The Ottoman Empire was at its height. The lands of Cathay were fabled, especially for rare and beautiful porcelain, which was highly prized and often mounted in silver or silver-gilt. Trade was being established with India. But it was from the Dutch East Indies, the lands of spice, that the real influence of the Orient came, though naturally via Holland.

Contact with the East was rapidly developing. Indeed, the King of Bantam sent an ambassador to Charles. His fantastic retinue must have delighted the King who himself kept the original 'Cockatoo' and tropical birds. Charles kept some of them in his dining-room. It is a short step, then, from 'Chinese' birds beside the table to cups and plates decorated with Chinese birds on the table.

8 From about 1670, therefore, concurrently with Dutch influence, Chinoiserie motifs appear. It remained in vogue for about fifteen years, reaching a peak of popularity about 1683. This decoration consisted of flat-chased Oriental figures in exaggerated attitudes walking in groves of strange plants. Imaginary birds fly above rocky gardens. The fabulous is evoked, yet in a curiously natural way. It is thought that one workshop was solely responsible for this style, which lent to the English court the image of the Chan. Charles II was no absolute monarch, but the Stuart dream remained in the silver landscapes of an imagined Peking. It was a dream that was to recur in the 18th century, and again in the 19th.

The Merry Monarch dispelled the rigorism of the Puritan Protectorate. Luxuries became respectable. Among the most popular items were double-handled (caudle) cups, used largely for spiced wines. A hot drink before a cold bed (or one heated with a silver warming-pan) was the rage.

Deep repoussé cups had been introduced from Holland before 1660. Usually with two handles, these were beautifully embossed and chased with flowers and foliage, and served to reassure the Restoration gentleman that he was again enjoying power and wealth.

Two-handled caudle cups, often used for mixtures of meat and vegetables as well as for hot wines, frequently had salvers to match, each about twelve inches across, with rims embossed with swirling foliage in which monkeys' and other animals' faces appear. This vitality complements the form of the cup. With its domical cover and finial, the cup presides over the salver, lending it a formal dignity. The clear form of the handles, moving in counterpoint with the ogee form of the cup, creates a balance. The vitality, however, is not that of the later Rococo.

Beer and cider were consumed in great quantities, and for the Restoration drinker tankards, growing in height as the reign proceeds, were eminently holdable.

Many were plain, but the fashion was for the lower half to be deeply embossed with either acanthus leaves or similar designs from Chinese porcelain. The London silversmith of acknowledged brilliance who used a mark consisting of *a goose in a dotted circle* is known to have 6, 12 made a number of the finest drinking vessels of this type in existence.

One of the most curious is the peg-tankard, with studs in a vertical row inside the container, probably as level-marks for drinking competitions, though this is uncertain. Some of them have three pomegranate feet and a matching thumbpiece, and were imported from Denmark or made in York or Hull under the influence of the Scandinavian trade.

Tankards were vertical and tapering, with a heavy handle and a flat lid with a thumbpiece, and either a stepped or a moulded base. Towards the end of the period the bodies became more shaped, and lids were given a dome-like moulding which eventually found a fuller expression during the 1730s. The handles have tongue-joints, and shield or lion thumbpieces, though in America the eagle sometimes occurs. Dolphins entwined were one of the most popular subjects for these thumbpieces.

By 1690 fluted surbases appear on tankards. The eye is invited to ripple its way from concave to convex, and the emphasis is on simplicity. The foundations were being laid for new designs in the reign of Queen Anne.

The first settlers in America were not anti-materialistic. Pious they were, but the Puritan idea that prosperity reflected divine favour persisted. Where trade thrived and commercial centres were established, there one finds a diversification of craftsmanship which at an early date included the silversmith. On the credit obtained from the export of the colonies' raw materials, merchants were quick to import English luxury goods. Curiously enough it was the lack of banks in the colonies which stimulated the American colonial silver industry. Savings were hoarded in hard coin which was often melted down and turned into plate. Readily identifiable if stolen, it could be reconverted in time of money scarcity, as long as a furnace capable of generating 1,000°C was available.

Early colonial silver displays the formative influence of the mother countries, especially England and Holland and, later, of the French Huguenots. Conditions and wealth varied from colony to colony, from town to country. In New England silversmiths were early members of the community, while in Virginia they arrived much later. The New Netherlands naturally saw the early supremacy of Dutch styles, while Pennsylvania was a thriving town before a silversmith appears. It was in Boston that the manufacture of silver first emerged.

When the settlers of Massachusetts Bay arrived, they brought with them a good deal of silver from England. By far the most common pieces extant are communion cups, which, however, may have begun life as ordinary drinking vessels. They reflect the styles current in London between 1629 and 1641, and were probably models for the earliest colonial silversmiths. With embossed Renaissance motifs, this stands in contrast to much Commonwealth silver.

A typical Boston cup from about 1639 is broader than its London counterpart of 1626. The base is flatter, and the baluster stem more robust. A common feature of mid 17th-century colonial silver is matting, a form of decoration without ostentation, the setting for a medallion in which initials could be inscribed. Decoration usually involved beading or foliate-chased stems, but was restrained. Silver of the period usually requires detailed stylistic analysis in order to date it in the absence of hallmarks and date letters. Inscriptions also allow approximate dates to be calculated, and for that reason are invaluable.

Effectively John Hull (1624–1683) was the first silversmith in Boston, though we know that one, John Mansfield, was there in 1634. John Hull was taught by his half-brother, Richard Storer, who himself had been trained in London after 1629 by James Fearne. It was Robert Sanderson (1608–1693), however, who pioneered the Boston silver industry. In 1638 he arrived in New England as a trained craftsman. Initially, therefore, Boston silver is directly influenced by the 'English' training of its earliest masters. Given that an indigenous silver industry arises between 1634 and 1650, one may presume that there was a significant demand for the metal. This was largely derived from Dutch, Spanish and

English coin. The quality naturally varied.

By 1652 a standard Mint had opened in Boston with Hull and Sanderson as its masters. They produced the now-prized pine and oaktree shillings and sixpences. By 1659 presentation church silver by Hull and Sanderson appears along with beakers, straight-sided and baseless. Matting is the only decoration, and they are reminiscent of London cups of about 1639. Both silversmiths were able to adapt from imported and earlier London silver to suit the requirements of the colonists. Their large communion cups display real craftsmanship and are amongst the most important early colonial silver. They cost about £5 or £7 in the 1660s. Less impressive, but more collectable, are the spoons made in this period by John Hull and John Coney (1655–1722). The bowls are oval and the handles either straight and rectangular or trefid-shaped with initials engraved on their underside. These are usually quite plain, and were made after about 1660.

Following the London fashion of the 1660s, Boston silver cups were flat-chased with flowers within strap-work or scroll panels. Later the panels disappear and the flowers run round the vessel in embossed friezes, and by 1700 fluted surbases appear. In the silver of both John Edwards and Jeremiah Dummer (1645–1718) plain areas alternate with embossed. Well defined shapes go hand in hand with naturalism.

Tazze and sweetmeat boxes are among the rarer objects. In the mid 1660s John Coney copied London models, with the bowls broken by cartouches banded by spiral flutes and acanthus leaves. Domed covers have gadrooned borders and occasionally serpent-like handles. Coney also made inkstands in which the lion thumbpieces featured on tankards are adapted as the feet.

In general the acanthus decoration which was so common on English silver of 1670–1695 never became popular in the colonies, where fluting was favoured. In this Jeremiah Dummer, a pupil of John Hull, took the lead, followed by his brother-in-law, John Coney.

If these men, along with Timothy Dwight, worked on beakers, cups, spoons and tankards with earnest skill, it was Edward Winslow (1669–1753) who brought flair to Boston silver. From the excellence of his work he may well have been trained abroad.

The plainer, less florid silver of Queen Anne's reign was welcomed in the colonies. A fillet of laurel marked the extreme of decoration on beakers, to which two handles could be added to make communion vessels. On the largest of them bands of fluting and narrow gadrooned borders give a sense of texture.

By 1664 the population of New Amsterdam, which in that year passed into English hands, was 34,000. Dutch traditions were to persist for a long time. Trading in tobacco and beaverskins, the Dutch colonists seem to have had very little coin at their disposal. By 1700, how-

ever, a flour exporting monopoly and a lively custom of privateering assured the wealth of New York. Officials and merchants alike seem to have co-operated with pirates who preyed on East Indies shipping off Madagascar, as we find in a letter from Governor Bellmont to the House of Lords regarding trade in 1698: ". . . by the confession of the merchants in the town they would have brought in a £100,000 in gold and silver".

This new wealth the New York burghers used in a typically Dutch way. Coveted glass and porcelain were imported, while the silver coin contributed to the furnishing of New York homes. Although a goldsmith is recorded as early as 1643, it is not before the last two decades of the 17th century that the silver industry in New York reaches significant proportions.

Many New York silversmiths from this period were Huguenots. They adapted the older Dutch motifs in much the same way as they modified their French (often provincial) designs to an English market. The most famous of these silversmiths was Bartholomew Le Roux, who died in 1713. His son, Charles, later became New York's official silversmith. Naturally Dutch influence remained dominant, as the names Jacob and Hendrich Boelen, and Jacobus van der Spiegel (1668–1708) would suggest. Their work remained conservatively Dutch with bands of strapwork and flat-chased floral decoration, and masks. Two-handled bowls were common instead of caudle cups, though Dutch silversmiths did adopt the tankard, which seems not to have been made in Holland.

The heaviness of embossed, engraved and cast ornamentation remains the outstanding stylistic feature of New York silver, though English shapes and details infiltrate the craft towards the beginning of the 18th century, leading to a simplification of design. Nevertheless, New York silver, compared with Bostonian and later with that of Philadelphia, remained more solid until well after 1750. New York silver tends to be thick-gauged and, in the case of cups and beakers, with strong moulding at the base, in contrast to the flat-chased or delicately moulded bases of Boston beakers.

Not all New York silver was decorated. Plain bowls of heavy silver made by Jacob Boelen and Cornelius Wynkoop are attractive, largely because of the hammered surface of their work. Tankards often were plain, though usually large. (Liquor consumption in the New Netherlands is shown by the fact that there seems to have been a ratio of one public house to every four houses.) New York tankards retained flat-topped lids and were without girdles and finials, unlike the tankards from New England or Pennsylvania. Indeed, it was 1750 before New York tankards adopt the baluster shape of their English counterparts. Thumbpieces are almost always of the corkscrew variety, a useful feature for identification. Sometimes the lids were decorated with a circular cartouche of leaves, enclosing the owner's cypher or monogram. Wynkoop, van der Spiegel, and Pieter van Dyck, however, produced more elaborately engraved designs. Occasionally medals and coins were inserted in

14

the lids of tankards, chiefly because of their historical or decorative qualities. Handles were frequently decorated with a cherub's head, though a man's head with a wig was almost as common.

In Pennsylvania and New Jersey, a tradition of silversmithing was early established. As in Boston and New York, the silversmiths tended to be civic gentlemen who supplemented their craft with an active interest in law, local government and militia. Gabriel Thomas's *Account of Pennsylvania and West New Jersey,* written in 1698, reports how plentiful silver was, largely because of the prosperity of the corn and livestock trade with the West Indies. This silver, however, was largely used to cover a balance of trade deficit incurred in trade with England. The colonies' money had been stabilised by 1722 in paper issues, thus freeing silver for the smith. By 1760 Philadelphia had overtaken Boston in population. William Penn himself had patronised local silversmiths, notably Johan Nys, Francis Richardson and Cesar Ghiselin. The latter was a Huguenot refugee, who is thought to have worked in Annapolis from 1715 to 1728, and who died in Philadelphia in 1733. Johan Nys was probably of French Protestant extraction who had gone to Holland and later to America. His tankards are strikingly like those made in New York, where in all probability he worked, before going to Philadelphia via New Jersey. Born in Ireland where he was trained in Cork, Philip Syng senior came to Philadelphia in 1714, and later moved to Annapolis. Along with his son Philip (1703–

1789) he produced a great amount of silver, and his two other sons and three grandsons followed in their footsteps. Richardson's son Joseph (1711–1784) and grandsons Joseph (1752–1831) and Nathaniel (1754–1827) also followed their fathers in contributing much excellent silver to Philadelphia throughout the 18th century. Other silversmiths of note were Elias Boudenot (1706–1770), Peter David (after 1739), William Ball (1759–1782), John Leacock (after 1751), and Edward Milne (1757–1773).

Based closely on English styles, Philadelphia silver was supplied to people of English descent. It also had to compete with the English silver which was imported by Edward Milne, amongst others. Quaker patrons usually preferred simple utility-orientated items. Tankards were usually with domed lids, but seldom had finials, and they adopted the baluster form of English models in the second half of the 18th century. Salt cellars, sauce- or creamboats of the middle of the century employ basic Rococo curves, but almost totally lack the moulded decoration of their European counterparts.

In Virginia and Maryland it is probably true to say that those who could afford silver bought it in London in exchange for tobacco. The southern colonies had few towns and no definite trading class. Only when Virginia and Maryland began to sustain a merchant class did silversmithing take root in Baltimore. By 1750 numerous advertisements for silversmiths appear in that city. George Aiken, Littleton Holland, J. Lynch and Lewis

15 A William and Mary teapot with cut-card decoration. Maker's mark: B.B., crescent below. London, 1685.

16 *left* A William III snuffers stand. Benjamin Bradford. London, 1698. *right* A Charles II caster. Maker's mark: W.B., mullet below. London, 1683.

Buichle, Charles L. Boehme and Christopher Hughes were the best-known makers of the second half of the 18th century, and their work naturally follows English styles.

Perhaps because of various impurities inherited from Spanish coin, silver in the South was hard and brittle. In 1743 and again in 1766 William Wright and Thomas You, both of Charleston, guaranteed their silver 'as good as sterling'. By 1730 at least nine silversmiths are recorded as working in Charleston, the outstanding commercial centre south of New York. Its international connexions probably explain the high number of French names, such as Moreau Sazzazin, and his son Jonathan, Francis Gaultier and Daniel Trezevant. The articles these silversmiths advertised seem to have comprised small items such as boxes, buckles, 'Tooth-Picker cases, Thimble and Needle cases, and cane Heads,' all highly collectable and indicative of the sophistication of the colonies in the years leading up to the War of Independence.

American silver, therefore, in the 17th and 18th centuries displays a wide variety of influences which reflect the political and commercial affairs of local colonial situations. Usually English styles predominate, except in New York, but to these are added the influence of French and European artisans with adaptations of their own designs and their adopted models. This forms the basis for the individuality of American silver, whose chief merit was clarity of design, simplicity and careful craftsmanship.

Queen Anne Silver

When Queen Anne succeeded William III in 1702, a reign began in which the monarchy developed a more restrained attitude to politics. As a monarch, Anne was to stress court procedure and protocol. The extreme formality usually associated with Louis XIV had come to England. She was first servant and defender of the people, a concept in keeping with the increase in the importance and the dignity of the individual. Man and his destiny were now understood in a more rational way. The atmosphere of high emotions was evolving into a sense of man's dignity. The collective security of nations and a desire to crush the power-lust of Louis XIV were the objectives of Anne's time. The mood was anti-French, rational and moderate.

Paradoxically it was from France and the skill of the French Huguenots that the new classicism in silverwork came.

As we have seen, the measured classicism of the French Grand Manner came from the classicism implicit in the Baroque philosophy. Even before 1685 Huguenots had arrived in London and tried to practise their art, much to the consternation of the London silversmiths, who repeatedly filed complaints with the Company of Goldsmiths against the 'Necessitous strangers'. Nevertheless it was the policy of Charles to aid those who were persecuted by his arch-enemy Louis. In spite of the professional jealousy which they encountered, men like Harache were enrolled in the Company as early as 1682. After 1689 Huguenot silversmiths came in increasing numbers. Indeed the Government paid £15,000 a year towards Huguenot relief. Slowly but surely this had an effect on silver.

The Glorious Revolution and the flight of the Catholic James II in 1688 was a landmark in British history. The time was ripe for a change. By 1700 the Dutch influence and Chinoiserie forms of decoration had all but vanished, except on heavily embossed wall-sconces and other formal plate. Nevertheless, vertical fluting and gadrooning persisted, especially on monteith bowls (so-called after an eccentric Scotsman named Monteigh), two-handled cups, and tankards. These conservative, and in many ways English, designs are often associated with the work of Seth Lofthouse, Samuel Wastell and others.

20, 21

The Huguenots took the classicism of the Baroque one stage further. Design is reduced to pure undecorated

form in the latter half of Queen Anne's reign and that of her successor George I. The English market was undergoing a miniature Puritan revolution away from things Carolean and Jacobean. The spirit of the Commonwealth silver is recast, but in a far more sophisticated form. If the Grand Alliance was stressing the political comity of nations, so English silver styles were part of an international trend. In Germany, Holland and Scandinavia silver design was also undergoing a purification based on principles derived from the Baroque.

Derived from French models, but international in scope, Queen Anne silver inherited an important logical aspect of the Baroque. The question of architectural form becomes that of the formal relationship of plain surfaces, one area juxtaposed with another. Since light can be deflected and reflected through an angle, these surfaces were related in such a way that now shape and texture is the product of form and light. This could be called the 'geometry of light'. The basic forms were the rectangle, the hexagon and the octagon. Since these are fundamentally linear, it is not surprising that the sense of line becomes all-important. Verticals are stressed, and silverwork tends to emphasise height. For example, handles on ewers tend to draw the eye upwards rather than outwards. Scrolls and S-shapes are now used to this effect, producing the elegance of the baluster form. Candlesticks, cups, and coffee pots conform to one or other of these geometric arrangements, or at least are given octagonal feet or stems.

Since heavy detail destroys pure line, even the bold castwork of the early Huguenots gives way to a lighter, more delicate strapwork. These motifs were either cast, cut, engraved or flat-chased. Accordingly, there was a revival of the art and importance of the engraver in the years 1700–1725.

When the line of a piece is of the greatest importance, it can be enhanced by cast features. It was a triumph of sensitivity and intuition that was to make the handles of vessels more complex, usually in a double-scroll form, while retaining a light simplicity. This is a trend that takes us into the ambiance of George II silver, and the later, more ambitious work of men like Paul de Lamerie.

Britannia Standard silver (1697–1720) was comparatively soft, owing to its lower content of base metal. The techniques, such as those used in the 17th century, which involved the stretching of the metal were discarded. Those which took only minimal amounts of silver from the piece, such as engraving, were encouraged. Naturally lavish embossing and repoussé-work, which require thin silver, all but disappear in favour of more substantial constructions.

The French custom of casting in high relief gave the Huguenot craftsmen an advantage. They knew how to cope with heavier forms of the metal. Apart from fluting, which was still raised from the surface by hammering,

17 A Queen Anne basting spoon. William Gamble. London, 1702.

18 A Queen Anne cup and cover with applied strapwork and gadroon borders. Pierre Harache junior. London, 1702.

19 A Queen Anne covered bowl with fluted decoration. John Boddington (died 1728). London, 1705.

 20 Seth Lofthouse, working about 1697 – about 1722.

 21 Samuel Wastell, working about 1701 – about 1721.

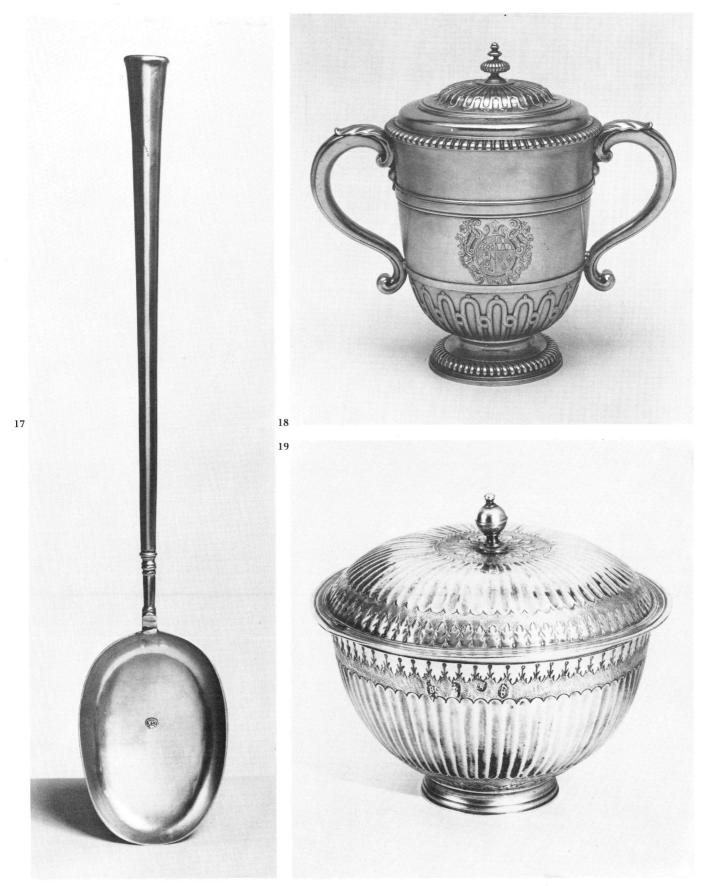

17

18

19

22 A Queen Anne covered beaker with
cutcard decoration. Joseph Ward. London,
1708.
23 A Queen Anne tea caddy. Thomas Ash.
London, 1711.

24 *left* A Queen Anne teapot. Thomas
Folkingham. London, 1713. *right* An early
18th-century cream jug. Unmarked. English,
about 1730. Victoria and Albert Museum,
London.

22

23

most of the ornamentation was now cast, greatly adding to the weight of the piece. Hence a new sculpturesque element was introduced to English silver. Masks, mouldings, flowerheads and other motifs are beautifully finished and replace lobes and free-style Dutch naturalism. Nevertheless, the English tradition of simplicity, especially on cups, tankards, teapots and coffee pots, persisted as a check on the more elaborate virtuoso brilliance of second-generation Huguenot silversmiths 25, 26 like Abraham Buteux (born 1698), or Paul de Lamerie 47 (1688–1751) who only in later years produced highly decorated pieces. Of course the inspiration worked the other way, and erstwhile plain silversmiths adopted the technical accomplishments of the Huguenots. For example, George and Francis Garthorne's workshops produced many magnificent 'Huguenot' pieces, though they may perhaps have employed French assistant 27 journeymen. So, too, did Anthony Nelme (died 1722) and 28 Benjamin Pyne (died 1732), all of whom were employed by William III and Queen Anne.

English taste and the new classicism produced the simplicity and formality of Queen Anne silver, while English laws and Huguenot ability reinforced its quality.

22

The Huguenot silversmiths brought with them the helmet-shaped ewers, soup tureens and écuelles. Though a few exist, silver teacups, unlike silver teapots and coffee pots, were never popular. Few of the Huguenot silversmiths, such as Isaac Liger, who came from Saumur, 29 Pierre Platel from Lorraine, and David Willaume senior 30 from Metz, had actually worked in France. James Fraillon 31 and John le Sage, however, apprenticed to Philip Roker 32 and Louis Cuny respectively, learnt their trade entirely in England. The influence of these men was therefore applied to the English market and tradition. They made a range of goods differing in type and degree of elaboration from those existing in French patternbooks of the period. Their work clearly shows the coalescence of Huguenot and English silverwork. If Queen Anne employed English silversmiths who had adopted English ways, George I and the Prince of Wales felt free to employ Fraillon, Philip Rollos, David Tanquery, or even de Lamerie's master, Pierre Platel. Royal patronage completed the process of naturalisation begun in 1681 with the Letters of Denization granted under the Great Seal of Charles II. In spite of the continual protestations of the English silversmiths, by 1710 the *'entente argente'* was

24

virtually complete. English silver had been revitalised. Its quality of design raised it above the parochial. The quality of its execution put it on a par with the best that France could produce. A new standard had been set for future silversmiths, and it is this which makes Queen Anne silver what it is, a triumph of skill and taste. It catches the predeliction of an age. What the eye sees, the heart understands. Silver had entered the orbit of the Ideal, and to its magic few can fail to succumb. An Apollonian dignity is born and bequeathed to the silver of future generations.

Apart from those still used as presentation pieces, standing cups of the Carolean variety were out of fashion, as were the individual wine cups, which were now made of the less expensive glass. Nevertheless, there was a steady evolution in the form and designs of the two-handled cup. These were now almost vertical in their lines. The older curve-sided cups had given way to Huguenot influence which can be detected in, for instance, the shape of the handles. Initially the French silversmiths employed harp-shaped handles, but these were superseded by a return of the traditional S-shaped examples.

As yet most of the English cups had ropework and fluting, while their Huguenot counterparts had the applied leaf and strapwork ornamentation that we have already described in connection with cutcard work (page 13). Some Huguenot masters, however, worked in a more English idiom, the best-known probably being Louis Cuny.

Another feature of the new cup designs was the domical cover, which replaces a flat lid. This maintains a sense of balance. By about 1704 a short stem was being introduced at the base of the cup, as we can see from the work of Platel or Rollos. A much favoured form of decoration around the lower sections of the cup was leaf and lanceolate strapwork which progressively became more ornate.

Naturally what applied to the two-handled cups could equally be applied to winecoolers, flagons, punchbowls and ewers. The handles of these were revolutionary. Generally speaking, if a cup or vessel has no girdle running around its middle, and if the sides are basically vertical, then it dates from about 1700. If, however, it is applied with a gadrooned or otherwise decorated moulding, then it probably belongs to a slightly later

33 A George I chocolate pot. Thomas Parr. London, 1715. Unlike coffee pots, chocolate pots have a covered aperture in the lid through which a stirring rod was placed.

34 A George I octafoil salver. Peter Archambo. London, 1722.

35 A Queen Anne octagonal teapot on lampstand. William Penstone. London, 1712.

33

34

35

36 George Garthorne, working about 1680—about 1727.

period, although this form of decoration was quickly displaced.

The monteith bowl was the product of Charles II's reign and it remained the item which embodied the more conservative features of English silverwork. The cherubs, the gadrooned or ropework girdles, and the vertical flutes were the cardinal features. While these persisted well into the 18th century, they were becoming less fashionable. There were now on the market the more sophisticated up-to-date bowls of the Huguenot craftsmen. Initially, the monteith bowl makers counteracted the competition by making it possible to remove the top rim, escalloped to hold wineglasses, so converting it to a punchbowl. The truth, however, was that they were still oldfashioned. The Anglo-French models were more elegant without the swing handles which hung from lion masks, but with the more 'trendy' decoration in the form of applied strapwork. Above all, they were of more 'classical' proportions. Punch must have been popular, for the largest of these has a capacity of four gallons.

Winecisterns and winefountains were also, by today's standards, of immoderate size. Indeed, the cisterns almost functioned as sinks, for we read that dishes were sometimes washed in them, but in effect they were gigantic winecoolers or icepails. Because of their bulk and melt-value, most of these have disappeared, although they were once reasonably common among the wealthier classes.

From those winecisterns which Pierre Harache was making in the 1690s we can see why the new styles were becoming popular. Beautiful simple lines are offset only by the restrained and tasteful addition of strapwork decoration. Compared to one made by George Garthorne 36 in 1694, decorated with broad lobes and raised on four massive lion paws, they are of a much more sophisticated nature—good enough reason for English silversmiths to follow the Harachian example. Such were Anthony Nelme or Benjamin Pyne, who could and did rival Rollos and Willaume in the execution of these large masterpieces.

More popular and more successful were the winecoolers. Designed to take only one bottle, they were a more domestic item altogether. They were often magnificent, incorporating the best features of Huguenot art. As useful pieces which were impressive when on display, they brought luxury and refinement of taste to the tables of their owners.

There was one item that the Huguenots had to adapt themselves to, namely the thoroughly English tankard. Wine rather than beer was the French drink, but in England there was a long tradition of beer-drinking. With their simple designs and good substantial handles, the tankards were overdue for re-definition. This the Huguenots did with masterly competence. What they found was virtually a plain tankard with tapering sides, flat lid, scroll handle, and perhaps flutes, gadroons, or a

37 Man and Child Drinking Tea. Painting by
an unknown American artist. About 1725.
The Colonial Williamsburg Collection.

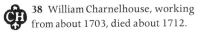

simple cable girdle. What they created was a vessel worthy of presentation.

Working on the basis of the cutcard decoration that was to be found on the best and most important of the English tankards, they modified the design by rounding the lower half of the vessel and by making the lid domical which in turn was presided over by a fine finial. A new skill was brought to the execution of the thumbpieces and the lion feet which had been older features. Again the more sophisticated Huguenot strapwork appears, although the fashion for fairly plain design persisted.

For those whose capacity for liquor was not as great as the tankard-man's there was the smaller mug, which had no lid and usually held about half a pint. These were extremely popular and large numbers are still extant.

During the period of Charles II, the toilet service had been developed, consisting of utensils for washing and grooming. Unfortunately most of these large services have been broken up. The most complete example from this period comprises 29 pieces, including a ewer, a silver-mounted looking-glass, pomade pots, two large and two small boxes, three caskets, two whisks and two clothes brushes, four square trays, a pair of candlesticks, two canisters, a pair of snuffers and a tray, and two glass jars with silver covers. This, the Treby service, now in the Ashmolean Museum, Oxford, was made by Paul de Lamerie in 1724. Others were made by such masters as David Willaume.

Unlike the Carolean ewer, which had been beaker-shaped on a truncated stem, the new ones were rather rounded, with a baluster foot and harp-shaped handles, or helmet-shaped with an open scroll handle. The latter became the standard, and naturally many examples were decorated with the classical strapwork.

The 18th century was the age *par exellence* of the coffee and tea houses, where business, politics and the arts were freely discussed. They were in effect the courts of the men of letters and the fashionable, venues for those who cared for the quality of life. Teapots were of various shapes. They had been introduced at the end of the 17th century, but these are now very rare. The first recorded example, now in the Victoria and Albert Museum, London, dates from 1670. Our first substantial encounter with them, however, is in the reign of Queen Anne. These could be circular or octagonal, with curved spouts which sometimes had monster heads at the tip.

35 Early teapots often had spirit lamps and stands, which seems to indicate that Anne and her subjects liked their tea stewed. These stands, however, have mostly disappeared. The beauty of the contrasting sides of the octagon made any decoration unnecessary. While the Huguenots did attempt to 'refine' the teapot with their usual strapwork decoration, this was not really successful. Purity of line and the perfect proportions were enough, and the teapot remained almost plain until the 1740s.

Samuel Wastell and William Charnelhouse were great 38 teapot makers, competing successfully with the French artisans.

While Anthony Nelme actually produced a square teapot, the goldsmiths of Edinburgh made teapots that were almost spherical.

Coffee pots of the last decade of the 17th century were usually of tapering cylindrical design, with a conical lid and a plain ebony handle set at right angles to the spout. By the early 18th century, however, the body had been rounded, almost as a prototype of the baluster shapes that were to become so fashionable. The lid was more domical than conical, and the lower half invited the applied or embossed decoration common at the time.

Generally speaking the tall tapering types are English, while the rounded are more in keeping with French taste. The former are extremely elegant and have often been copied. Even today coffee pots based on originals by John Fawdery or William Lukin are found. The design is the same, but there the comparison ends, for today's versions are thin, rather too perfectly stamped-out constructions that lack both the rich blue lustre and density that one associates with the earlier work. They remain productions rather than creations.

By the end of the 17th century columnar candlesticks were considered oldfashioned. These hollow forms had stood on square or octagonal feet, and only rarely had the baluster form been used.

With the advent of the new, more sculpturesque element, candlesticks from the turn of the century were almost always cast. Made in sections, they invited a more elaborate treatment of both foot and stem. Quickly the baluster-shape superseded earlier models, and the stems were decorated with gadrooning, though on some of the best examples shells and masks appear. The counterchanged facets of the octagonal bases were alternately decorated, while some makers preferred a circular foot which rose to cast knops and shoulders gadrooned to taste. Basically the octagonal or hexagonal baluster-shape dominates the period of Queen Anne to George II.

Chamber candlesticks also appeared, usually with short stems and circular pans with handles, and fitted with detachable conical extinguishers, while tapersticks (a smaller version of the table candlestick) also occur.

Such articles, along with an immense selection of other items, mark the sophistication, the elegance of life in Queen Anne's reign and under her first two Hanoverian successors. The age of Dryden, Swift and Pope was to remain the epitome of taste and culture until the advent of the more precocious Rococo style. Even then English silver never quite lost the magic of the measured classicism of Queen Anne silver. In adapted forms it has proved itself to have perennial appeal.

The Rococo

40 As early as 1701 William Lukin had felt impelled to bring relief to the classical lines of a chocolate pot by creating a 'double-chin' effect at the base of its spout. This was a token of things to come.

By the 1720s Paul de Lamerie was producing pieces which preserved the classical forms, but were decorated with applied mouldings, lion masks, free scrollwork, and shell motifs. These additions could give the appearance of asymmetry. Nevertheless, the poise remains classical. It is but a small step to the largely French-bred style called Rococo.

Essentially Rococo art is based on natural forms – rocks, shells and waterfalls. Since prehistoric times and particularly in classical antiquity, such things had symbolised the vitality and mystery of the forces of nature, and Raphael, Giovanni da Udine and Alberti in Italy and Primaticcio in France designed gardens, grottoes and sculptures which, with all their classical motifs, evoked the pagan half-demonic elements in nature. Inside the form of beauty was the beast of dynamism. Rugged rocks, shells and writhing scrolls spoke of natural forces which slowly and blindly change everything. It was these forces which Michelangelo's figures had massively expressed.

Just as Michelangelo in his late work transformed the Platonic ideal of beauty, seen in, for instance, his 1498 *Pietà*, into the Dionysian vision of muscular strength within the human figure, so Rococo art investigated the arcane energy which the Baroque forms had concealed. To that extent Rococo art tried to come to terms with the energy of natural shapes.

In terms of silver, naturalistic decoration was allowed to completely dictate the form of the piece. In a real sense, the piece *is* the decoration, forming a new ambiguous reality, which at its worst is mere whimsy, at its best an example of the potency of natural accretion. The amalgams that ensue are both natural and unreal. On one level the artist is true to the natural form of shell, rock and stream, at another he is true to the force of nature itself. Rococo remains a study of the naturally unnatural.

In England, silverwork, already relieved of its plainness by the genius of Paul de Lamerie, only adopted Rococo elements rather than wholeheartedly embracing what was a commanding art movement in France, south

Germany, northern Italy and Austria. English silver was influenced by, but remained peripheral to, the Rococo movement in general. The exuberance of Watteau, Boucher and Tiepolo did not take root in Britain. What was adopted were those features of design and decoration which could modify established forms rather than create a new style. Rococo was a sophisticated attempt to make formal styles more lively. It always remained a rather 'un-English' phenomenon.

An early acceptance of elaborately engraved cartouches for armorials augered well for the development of a taste for detailed decorative effects. As early as 1700 Pierre Harache was making pieces which display superbly engraved architectural strapwork festooned with ribbon-tied husks, formal foliage, birds, cherubs, female masks and large scallop-shells. Such stylistic trends came from engravers like Simon Gribelin (1661–1733) who came from France to England in 1680. Under Huguenot influence, Régence decoration was featured on English silver, though in practice it took a more subdued form. Flat-chased areas of decoration between salver bases and borders appear, along with oblong panels of diaperwork and arabesques. The fact that such decorative details, taken from French silver, appear in the work of Willaume, George Wickes, Peter Archambo and Paul de Lamerie 41, tells us that tastes were again changing. This is most noticeable in the applied sections of domestic items like coffee pots and salvers. Whereas these had formerly been plain, straight or gracefully curved, they were now decorated with leaf-capped scrolls as handles, or small scrolls interspersed with shell motifs as borders. Applied work evolved from simple cutcard designs into strapwork with applied beading, raised husks, crossed scrolls and classical profiles. By the 1730s caryatids and festoons of naturalistic detail appear, and a point is reached where, in the words of N. M. Penzer, 'It is by no means easy to determine where one style ends and another begins.' English silver was now ready for the Rococoesque work of Paul de Lamerie (1688–1751). Formerly this master had worked with great success in the style of Queen Anne and George I. Indeed, his early work ranks among the best of its style, putting him on a par with silversmiths like Simon Pantin senior, an apprentice of 43 Pierre Harache, Augustine Courtauld, who was master to another good craftsman Edward Feline, and David 44 Willaume. With his brilliant technique Paul de Lamerie not only mastered the subtleties which Huguenot standards demanded of the metal but he soon turned his attention to the challenging art of Rococo which demanded the full range of virtuoso craftsmanship. From 1712, when de Lamerie had entered his mark at the Goldsmiths' Hall, until a year before his death in 1751, he built and maintained a reputation for the finest silver workshop in London. Indeed the de Lamerie œuvre is almost a synonym for the best of English Rococo.

40 William Lukin, working from about 1699, died after 1755.

 41 George Wickes, working from about 1720, died about 1770.

42 Peter Archambo, working from about 1720, died 1767.

43 Simon Pantin senior, working from about 1701, died about 1729.

44 Edward Feline, working from about 1721, died about 1753.

45

Paul de Lamerie's work shows the evolution of the Rococo style through the elaboration of Huguenot and 47 Régence-like motifs. For example, small milk jugs which he produced in the 1730s, and which were also made by George Wickes, are decorated with the popular Régence flat-chased diaperwork, scrolls and husk motifs. Four volute supports, however, extend in graceful curves from an upper terminal made to suggest a blind mask. A nose is evident and a leg seems to protrude from a mouth, but the remainder of the design is lost in three carefully worked scrolls which hide the remaining features. The handle rises from the back of the lip forming itself into a vulture-like head, and in turn the handle continues out of its beak. The strange unnatural realism with its grotesque effect is highly reminiscent of the work of the Dutch Mannerists like Adam van Vianen who, as we have seen, worked during the first half of the previous century.

A chocolate pot by de Lamerie, made in 1738, has an elongated pear-shaped body decorated with three panels bordered by massive flattened scrolls. Each contains a scene of romantically treated cherubs in a country setting with trees in the distance. Most unusually, the body is raised on three scrolling supports. The effect is distinctly Rococoesque. Such styling was to remain in vogue in England for the next ten years.

Makers other than Paul de Lamerie worked in the same vein, though whether with the same flair is doubtful.

The most successful was Charles Kandler whose tea 48 kettle dating from the years 1727–1737 is a masterpiece of invention. Now in the Victoria and Albert Museum, this piece has a spherical body with applied mythological scenes representing the triumph of Neptune and Ariadne. The whole composition is draped in seaweeds and shells. The spout is particularly fine, comprising a fully modelled triton blowing a conch-shell as he rises from the waves. The conception may well be based on Italian or German Mannerist etchings of the mid 16th century. In short, it displays the three key elements of Rococo art: an asymmetrical amalgam of natural objects like shells, a grotesque quality, and a mythological theme derived from antiquity or the Renaissance.

In a sauceboat made by John Eckfourd in 1746 one sees 49 the more purely naturalistic aspect of Rococo. The oblong body is encased by scrolling foliage which contains two scenes depicting a ram in a rustic setting. The tapering stem suggests a spray of waves against unyielding rocks. Undoubtedly these elements are Rococoesque, but the handle, modelled as a spaniel with its tongue panting into the sauceboat, points forward a hundred years to Victorian naturalism. It is a fanciful, even sentimental addition, superb in its realism but lacking a grotesque quality found in the best continental Rococo where natural objects coalesce and grow in weird groupings. The dog is whimsical rather than exotic, and the whole piece shows how domestic Rococo silver in England

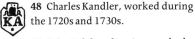

46

echoed rather than rivalled its continental counterpart.

As the Rococo style began to lose its momentum, English silver remained Rococo only in as much as bundles of fruit and vegetables, flowers and leaves, like the dog, were given Rococoesque settings. Indeed, a new form of Chinoiserie appeared, fascinating the designers as it had done in the 1670s. If the term 'Naturalistic-Chinese-Rococo' is meaningless, it shows an extraordinary eclecticism at work in English silver.

Usually cast or chased in low relief, these Chinese 51 motifs were inspired by the work of French painters like Boucher. Chinamen, however, appear, not among exotic palms, but whimsical scrolling fantasies, with exotic flowers meandering in and out of crevices. By the 1760s coffee pots had assumed new baluster or bellied shapes which were often decorated with such scenes. One particularly interesting design is for a rectangular tea caddy made in 1764. Roughly in the form of a pagoda, it is chased with Oriental figures. The foliage weaves itself into the semblance of a ruined gazebo, and the whole scene is contained within borders of applied valancing. The corners are filled with free-standing columns overgrown with trailing leaves.

Such flowers and leaves were very popular. If de Lamerie had made them they would probably have been applied decoration, but the average sugar bowls and

47

50 A George II Rococo candlestick. Anne Craig
& John Neville. London, 1740.

tea caddies, salvers, tankards and wine ewers snatch at
Rococo by means of a few scrolls or shells rather than by
the painstaking creativity of the true Rococo craftsman.
Though the tea caddies of Samuel Taylor and the coffee 52
pots and cups of Aymé Videau, who had been apprenticed 53
to David Willaume junior in 1723, are of considerable
merit, they display a truncated, rather superficial
understanding of the true capacities of Rococo art. It was
this quasi-Rococo work which was to be the model for the
chasers and casters of the period 1820–1855, as they
sought to rework old silver as well as new into what they
thought was an imitation of genuine Rococo work.
Naturally such 'Rococo' effects bore little resemblance
to the earlier chasing of mid 18th-century craftsmen. In
fact, what was achieved was a reinterpretation of
decorative naturalism with Rococo trimmings.

Engraving as a simple form of decoration was also
favoured now, just before the Neo-classical period. It
occurs frequently on circular tea caddies, or those
made in imitation of tea chests. The otherwise plain bodies
are engraved with delicate borders of scrolling leafage
within matted or hatched areas, while the interior of
these designs are sometimes filled with a single Chinese
character. It should be remembered that great quantities
of Chinese porcelain, made expressly for the European
market, were arriving, and the Chinese motifs and types
of decoration were of course reflected in the silversmiths' output.

Popular items of domestic plate (other than those
required by the great houses and royalty, when size and
function outstripped the needs of the ordinary consumer)
included a newcomer to the silversmiths' repertoire, the
épergne or centrepiece. Originally introduced in the
first twenty years of the 18th century, it consisted of a
central basket, and branches for further baskets or
candleholders. It was usually supported on four curved
legs. Paul de Lamerie made a number of these including
the Newdegate centrepiece of 1743. So, too, did Augustine
Courtauld, and perhaps the most fantastic of all is one in
the Queen's collection made by George Wickes in 1746
to a design by William Kent which had been published
in 1744. This piece has now been considerably altered to
suit tastes of succeeding generations. Other, more
modest makers, such as Thomas Pitts, and William
Plummer who specialised in pierced-work, were also
makers of épergnes. These were produced in significant
numbers during the 1760s and the following twenty
years.

Other items of domestic plate at the period include the
coffee pot, teapot, salver, and cruet stands, usually of a
cinquefoil plan with ringholders for a set of three casters
and two silver-mounted glass bottles. Tea kettles were
usually of a spherical or inverted pear-shape, while
sauceboats were oval. Supported on three scroll feet,
they feature flying-scroll leaf-capped handles. Mustard

51 A George III tea caddy with chased
Chinoiserie decoration. Pierre Gillois.
London, 1766. Victoria and Albert Museum,
London.

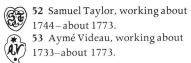

52 Samuel Taylor, working about
1744 – about 1773.
53 Aymé Videau, working about
1733 – about 1773.

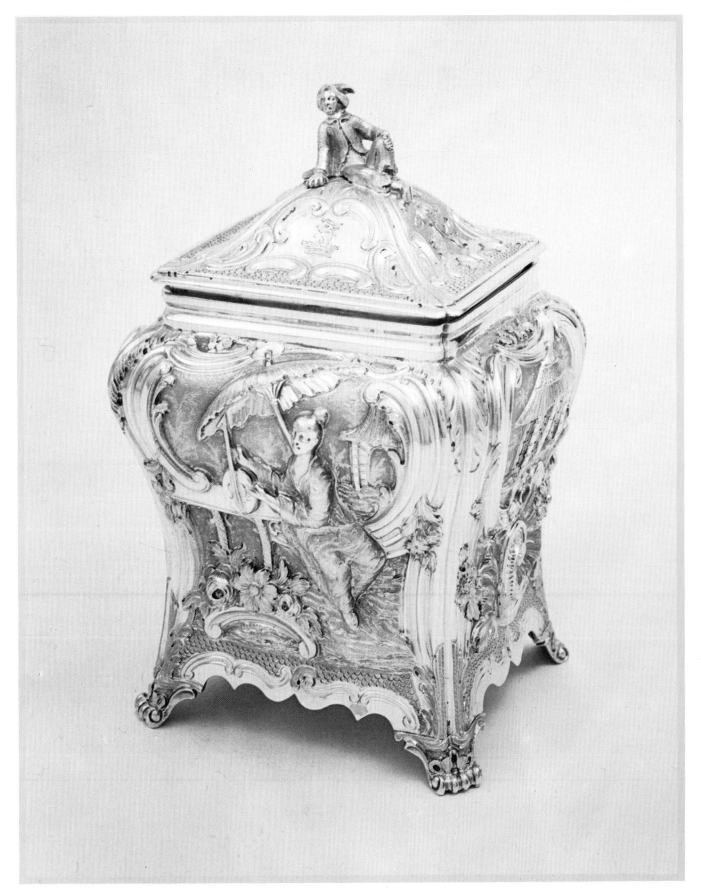

54

55

56 A George III pierced and engraved mustard pot. Francis Spilsbury junior. London, 1769. Fitzwilliam Museum, Cambridge.

57 A George II tankard. William Shaw & William Priest. London, 1753.

58 Paul Crespin, 1694–1770.

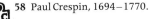

56

57

pots were generally plain cylindrical, pierced with quatrefoils or scrolls. Candlesticks either had modelled figure stems, or square bases and fluted baluster stems decorated with stylised shells. Naturally, the whole range of table silver was manufactured, including the newly accepted fish and cake slice. The blades of these were usually pierced and engraved with fish, fountains and birds.

This period, too, was one when an increasing amount of glass was made. Cheap and easily replaced, it suited the growing popularity of foreign wines. Silver mugs and tankards for the most part tended to be larger and made to a more traditional design. Indeed, very few tankards and mugs of any interest were made after about 1760.

The Rococo period in England begins, therefore, with the artistry of Paul de Lamerie, Paul Crespin and the **58** other craftsmen already mentioned, only to end in the rather commonplace multiplication of scrolls, shells, leaves and other natural objects. English Rococo becomes more of a fashionable genre than a genuine revolution in taste. Soon the intelligentsia, who had originally esteemed it, was to disdain it because of its very lack of intelligibility. At the end of the day its decorative effect, concealing an English taste for a more direct naturalism, became redundant simply in terms of its own monotony. The door was open for a return to a more considered appraisal of proportion, harmony and balance, as well as a more profound treatment of natural objects. The former was about to arrive in the guise of Neo-classicism. The latter had to wait another fifty years until the age of Adam had in turn exhausted itself.

Adam Silver

The second half of the 18th century was a time of enormous social upheaval in England. The Industrial Revolution was well under way, bringing new social problems and political consequences. Although the squirearchy largely maintained its privileged position, it was threatened by the rise of a new class of merchants. These selfmade men, the inventors, the manufacturers and successful artisans, aspired to a way of life which would proclaim their success. Through the display which wealth afforded they could feel compensated for their lack of social standing or political power. The silver industry more than ever had to cater for a market which required a greater variety of domestic items as well as a constant flow of pieces which affirmed a man's arrival in society or his success in business. Silver was now seen not primarily as the prerogative of the upper classes, but the aspiration of those who could afford to display their own estimation of themselves. Hence the growing popularity of presentation and domestic plate after 1760.

The Industrial Revolution was creating a new meritocracy in which a premium was placed on education, knowledge, inventiveness, resourcefulness and ability to adapt. The old society felt threatened. The new society was still unsure of itself. The former found in the works of classical antiquity the reassurance of an orderly society. The latter found in the stoic concept of virtue justification for business skill and self-aggrandisement.

The growing pace of industrial change and the rise of a new middle class with democratic ideals combined to create an atmosphere in which an art that expressed achievement could flourish. This search for security concealed heroic longings. For all its classical refinement, Adam silver was to satisfy these elements, but above all it was to be a style more pervasive than anything in the history of silver. The new manufacturing centres of Birmingham and Sheffield provided the means of spreading it far and wide. The classical dream was essentially the product of a new technological society searching for a style of life that was more a dream than a reality. As had often happened from the Renaissance onwards, designers, artists, manufacturers and craftsmen were to turn to the ideals of Greek art and the domestic practicality of the Roman Republic for its inspiration. For forty years silver was to be marked, as it were, with the letters 'S.P.Q.R.' Perhaps the appeal of Adam silver

was precisely this: it bestowed an ideal identity on its owners. Such was the appeal of 'the antique' that original creations were quite unpopular. In the diary of Sophie v. la Roche for 1786, we find the following entry:

> 'We visited Messrs. Jeffries' silver store . . . whose stock must be worth millions. It was all illuminated . . . full of sparkling gold and silver moulds and vessels . . . Those antique, well-preserved pieces, so Mr. Jeffries said, often find a purchaser more readily than the modern.'

Silver, as it were, encouraged its owner to play the role of Caesar, though he were in reality a coalmerchant or bridgebuilder.

The Neo-classical revival known as the 'Adam style' in England succeeded the Rococo very rapidly. Within the ten years up to 1770 the transition was completed. This new style owed its existence in a large measure to the architect Robert Adam (1728–1792) and his brother James.

Between 1754 and 1758 Adam had visited Italy where he studied the ruins and remains of classical antiquity. Much groundwork had already been done to prepare the public for the classical style. The excavations of Herculaneum and Pompeii, begun in 1738 and 1755 respectively, had received wide publicity, while illustrated publications had been issued by scholars and excavators. These included four volumes by P. V. d'Hancarville describing the collection of Sir William Hamilton, who had been the British envoy in Naples. Works by G. B. Piranesi, Comte de Caylus, Robert Wood, J. D. le Roy and J. J. Winckelmann were all published between 1748 and 1767. Caylus's *Recueil d'Antiquité* particularly influenced Josiah Wedgwood, while J. F. de Neufforge's *Recueil Elémentaire d'Architecture* was the source for Neo-classical motifs which was probably formative of Adam's concept of design. This work shows how comprehensive the style truly was, covering everything from furniture and domestic objects to interior decoration and architecture. By 1761 Robert Adam had systematically worked out his classical style, as can be seen in Osterley Park, near London, which he had rebuilt for Sir Francis Child. He undertook designs for furnishings, fittings and accessories. A few of his designs for silver are preserved at Sir John Soane's Museum, Lincoln's Inn Fields, London, and can in some cases be linked with pieces of manufactured plate.

The inspiration for silver design, although from Graeco-Roman art, was not from Graeco-Roman silver. The great hoards of classical plate, notably the treasures of Bernay and Boscoreale, were yet to be discovered. Instead design was based on bronze and marble articles, mostly on vases. These could be admirably adapted for

59 A George III épergne. Thomas Pitts.
London, 1767.

60 A George III salver. Edward Capper. London, 1772. The fine quality of the engraving is an interesting feature.

VERITAS ODIUM PARIT

cups, soup and sauce tureens, and tea and coffee urns. More imagination and invention, however, had to be used in the production of teapots and coffee pots, milk jugs, wine ewers and candlesticks. Hence the importance of understanding the principles of design embodied in the classical objects that were recovered. Formulae for proportions and codes of decoration were worked out. It was thought that if these were stringently adhered to, a truly classical object would be produced. In this way designers undertook to 'invent' articles in the Neoclassical style. It also explains why some items are faithful copies of archaeological finds, while others display a licence and a liberty which shows that silversmiths were in fact more creative and less purist in their work than is commonly imagined. It was academic fussiness over form and decoration which led to the trivialisation and eventually the sterility of the Adam style, though as we shall see other factors were also involved.

The simplicity of the Adam design was admirably suited to the new techniques of production which were revolutionising the market. As early as 1743 Thomas Boulsover, a buttonmaker, developed a technique of fusing silver to copper, producing what is now known as Sheffield plate. Though not hallmarked, this provided 63 a form of plated metal which could be rolled, hammered and punched into any shape desired without losing its covering of silver. From its application in the Sheffield button industry, the technique was expanded, and then developed by Matthew Boulton (1728–1809) in the 1760s. Himself a buttonmaker and silver piercer, Boulton's partnership with John Fothergill was the 62 foundation of a business enterprise which brought the silver industry into the main stream of the Industrial Revolution. From 1764 onwards they untiringly copied rare designs, marrying quality to quantity in their Soho factory at Birmingham. So the era of mass-production was born.

38

61 Two George III tea urns. *left* James Young. London, 1775. *right* Andrew Fogelberg. London, 1771.

MB IF **62** Matthew Boulton & John Fothergill, firm's mark entered in 1773.

Horace Walpole (1717–1797), in a letter to Mrs Montague in 1760, makes an interesting comment:

'As I went to Lord Stafford's I passed through Sheffield, which is one of the foulest towns in England, in the most charming situation, where there are 22,000 inhabitants making knives and scissors. They remit eleven thousand pounds a week to London. One man there has discovered the art of plating copper with silver. I bought a pair of candlesticks for two guineas, they are quite pretty.'

Boulton's contacts were not confined to men of discrimination in the arts, but to men with international business connexions like John Fothergill, and men of the genius of James Watt with whom he went into partnership in 1775. Watt's presence led to the widespread use of the steam engine. Consequently methods of production were begun which could make Walpole's two-guinea candlesticks even cheaper. Stamping and piercing were also carried out in a swift simple manner by improved fly-punches and without the aid of craftsmen. Roughly finished component parts were also made, then sold to independent workmen all over the country. It is possible, therefore, to find in provincial Neo-classical pieces identical features, for the average silver item was an assemblage rather than an individually executed craft piece. J. F. Hayward's suggestion that English silver of the Adam style 'is of unequal merit owing to the introduction of industrial methods' is to this extent correct. Thousands of stereotyped articles flooded the market. Teapots, coffee pots and oval cake baskets were easily assembled from thin sheets of silver, or spun on machines to form the body of the article. The ultra simple designs were naturally favoured by most manufacturers. To these it was easy to apply the rather beady classical motifs and insipid festoons.

Matthew Boulton's connexions ranged from Robert Adam to James 'Athenian' Stuart and John Flaxman

senior, whose son in turn worked for that other Neo-classical entrepreneur Josiah Wedgwood (1730–1795) and later as modeller to the royal goldsmiths Rundell, Bridge & Rundell. Boulton had an opportune sense of taste. In a letter to a relative, he states:

> 'ye present age distinguishes itself by adopting the most Elegant ornaments of the most refined Grecian artists, I am satisfy'd in conforming thereto, & humbly copying their style, & makeing new combinations of old ornaments without presuming to invent new ones.'

This succinctly shows how Neo-classicism was adapted to mass-production and to popular taste. It also shows how creativity was hampered by a sense of conformity, while perhaps the very lack of presumption that Boulton mentions contained the seeds for the style's decay. The drawbench and precision techniques gave the silversmith an unparalleled opportunity to be novel in design, but were not fully exploited. The Greek and later the Imperial Roman prototypes were endlessly copied to the point of monotony. A style, however, that is born and

lives by democratic appeal will also fall under democratic opinion, and the work of Boulton's factory marks the beginning of complete availability of silver for all classes. Henceforth the designer had to be more market-conscious. Increasingly before a style could be embraced a public had to be informed, and without public approval the artist would be considered either eccentric or revolutionary. From this point onwards the silversmith has two options, the option of being market-minded or being a creative artist. This was the tension with which the next generation of silversmiths had to live and which it had to resolve.

The Neo-classical style was also adopted on the continent. As Matthew Boulton says, he had 'establish'd a Correspondance in almost every mircantile Town in Europe . . . ' In France painters such as David had evolved a style which displays the heroic element of the movement. History painting, on an undomestic scale, was considered the epitome of art. While France adapted the new styles in silver before becoming preoccupied with her own troubles in the Revolution, the Rococo style remained dominant. The keenest

64 A George III silver-gilt covered vase. John Arnell. London, 1772. Contemporary black basalt covered vase, of the same design, by Wedgwood. Victoria and Albert Museum, London.

countries to take up the style were Portugal, which had friendly relations with Britain, and Scandinavia. Although in the 1770s Britain lost her American colonies, British trading influence remained intact, and Bostonian fashion-consciousness still followed the London modes. As in the early years of the 18th century, silver design in America was still subject to the influence of England. Indeed, firms such as Richardson's, a Quaker family of silversmiths from Philadelphia, are known to have imported stock from London. The selfconsciously elegant and trivial forms of popular English silverwork were slavishly followed. Vase-shaped coffee pots, oval salvers and the whole range of domestic wares in this reinterpreted classical style were produced in quantity.

Notable American makers of this period include Paul Revere (1735–1818), the son of a Huguenot silversmith Apollos Rivoire (1702–1754) who had settled in Boston in 1715. Revere, who eventually opened a bell and cannon factory in Boston in 1796, was as content as his contemporaries to imitate the imported Neo-classical style. His revolutionary interest does not seem to have extended to his artistic imagination.

Philadelphia, which declined considerably in importance after outbreaks of yellow fever in 1793 and 1798, was the hometown of such silversmiths as Abraham Dubois, Richard Humphreys, James Black and Christian Wiltberger. While these and other craftsmen were essentially provincial in outlook, some of their products are of rich interest. An historic tea and coffee set of about 1799, attributed to Wiltberger, for instance, displays a subtle understanding of proportion in relation to light. The monotony of the vase-shape is dispelled in a series of fluted panels which break up the light immediately below borders of roundels and bright-cut leafage. This set, now on view at the New York Metropolitan Museum of Art from the collection of Mrs Edwin A. S. Lewis, is thought to have been the gift of George Washington to his stepdaughter Eleanor. Not surprisingly Neo-classical silver, with its early Federal associations, has remained popular in America to the present day.

Much Neo-classical silver is of a rather poor quality, largely because of the mass-production techniques. The

65 A George III candelabrum. William Pitts & Joseph Preedy. London, 1794.
66 A George III coffee pot. Richard Morrison and Benjamin Stephenson. London, 1774.

67 A George III silver-gilt jardinière and stand. John Wakelin & William Taylor. London, 1787/89.

68 Henry Chawner, working from about 1785, died 1851.
69 Hester Bateman, 1709–1794.
70 Benjamin Stephenson, working about 1774–about 1779.

designs for these were occasionally pirated and in meaner hands were simplified and standardised to facilitate reproduction. Furthermore, the success of mass-production forced many small independent silversmiths with their craft skills out of business. The commercial success of the Birmingham and Sheffield companies, which absorbed English silversmiths and continental designers, relied on a mean between two extremes: excellent craftsmanship and machine-made uniformity. Matthew Boulton, for example, at one time had a staff of some six or seven hundred.

Many individual craftsmen did, however, thrive. **68** Such were Henry Chawner (died 1851) and Hester **69** Bateman (1709–1794). The work of the latter undoubtedly is representative of the way in which Neo-classicism was romanticised, even misunderstood. Festoons of bright-cut flowers, more in the Rococo tradition of Aymé Videau, Samuel Taylor or Phillips Garden, appear as poor imitations of the more considered **70, 71** work of Benjamin Stephenson or Wakelin & Taylor. The delicate work of Hester Bateman, however, was excellently suited to small items like wine labels and sugar tongs. Notable London silversmiths of the period **72, 73** include James Young, John Schofield, whose candlesticks and cake baskets display workmanship of the **74** highest order, and the firm of Carter, Smith & Sharp.

It was the ruling classes, however, with their extensive connexions on the continent, who still continued to be the heaviest users of silver. It was for them that the London craftsmen produced their finest pieces. Even Matthew Boulton, who had succeeded in being patronised by the Crown as well as by some of the great houses, was producing a range of quite outstanding items. These included a fine range of vase-shaped jugs, one of which is in the Museum of Fine Arts, Boston, tureens, candlesticks and other ornamental domestic plate. George III, it must be admitted, did not order plate on a grand scale, for his tastes were quiet, a feature which his domestic life reflected. The royal goldsmith **75** at this time was Thomas Heming who died at an advanced age at the turn of the century. Consequently little costly royal plate was required or ordered at this period. It was not until the Prince Regent, later George IV, started ordering expensive plate that the full swing of excitement pervaded the silver industry as it had done following the Reformation. Basically this change occurred after the Prince of Wales was set up in his own establishment at Carlton House in 1781. He did not, however, order plate on a large scale until after 1800.

Classical motifs play a very important part in this and the succeeding period in silver, and features that were quick to make their appearance included acanthus leafage, laurel sprays, vines, oak and acorn motifs, anthemions (honeysuckle), husks, festoons of flowers and leaves, fruit, drapery swags, skulls of rams, human

65
67

71 John Wakelin & William Taylor, successors to John Parker & Edward Wakelin, partnership 1776 – about 1792.

72 James Young, formerly in partnership with Orlando Jackson, working about 1774 – about 1790.

73 John Schofield, formerly in partnership with Robert Jones, working about 1778 – about 1793.

74 Richard Carter, Daniel Smith & Robert Sharp, firm's mark entered in 1777.

75 Thomas Heming, working from about 1737, died 1795/1801.

76 Andrew Fogelberg & Stephen Gilbert, in partnership 1780 – 1793.

77 Daniel Smith & Robert Sharp, in partnership about 1763 – 1778.

or half-human masks, dolphins, fretwork, key patterns, Vitruvian (continuous-wave) scrolls and fluting. Bright-cut, a common feature at this period, was a form of engraving done with a polished spatula-shaped tool which gouged out the metal. It left a clean bright surface or surfaces intended to catch the light. It was particularly popular on hosts of flimsy teapots, coffee pots, teapot stands, milk jugs, trays and salvers which were not of sufficiently inspired quality to do without this very effeminate form of decoration. Reducing most pieces to an offensively flashy level, bright-cut nevertheless continued in a debased form until the early years of the 19th century, though its popularity rapidly declined after 1790. Silver-gilt at this period was invariably reserved for the most important items.

Another form of decoration, which appears on the work of the London-based Swedish silversmith Andrew Fogelberg (who was for a time in partnership with Stephen Gilbert) and on the early work of his apprentice Paul Storr, is the applied cast cameo which had been inspired by discoveries of classical intaglios and cameos. These may well have been supplied to Fogelberg from originals by James Tassie (1735 – 1799), a neighbour, who did similar work for Josiah Wedgwood. Indeed, many similarities exist between Wedgwood porcelain and silver at this period. For instance, the fluted ovoid silver-gilt covered vase, made by John Arnell in 1772, resembles certain pieces of contemporary Wedgwood. It is applied with ribbon-tied drapery festoons, and on either side appears a grip or handle in the form of a modelled satyr mask. The cover is surmounted by a putto, while the square pedestal base is further decorated with drapes. Wedgwood vases of almost exactly the same design exist in black basalt. The pervasive Adam style was affecting everything from furniture to door handles, from drinking vessels to country houses.

Presentation plate also grew in importance at this time. One interesting example is the magnificent cup made by Daniel Smith and Robert Sharp of London from a design by Robert Adam, for the Richmond Races of 1770. Here the classical vase form of the body is pulled out, as it were, by the action of two beautifully formed caryatid handles. These are attached to the body by wingtips at the top, and in a series of tightly wrapped spirals at the bottom. The body itself is supported on a spirally fluted pedestal base, and the lower part of the bowl emerges from two rows of stiff leafage. Above this calyx appear two oval reserves, one of which contains a cameo-like racing scene within a small trail of vines and bunches of grapes. Above the ovals a further band of equestrian figures is chased in low relief. The cup is topped by a capstan-shaped cover decorated with stiff leafage caught at the waist of the spool by a band of Greek key pattern. Above this rises a finely wrought foliate finial.

Engraving on silver during the latter part of the 18th century plays a less important part. Armorials, however, were contained in loose cartouches whose nature dispelled the asymmetry of Rococo designs. Instead order and quietness reign in the form of husk festoons surrounding a simple shield which may well be flanked by crossed laurel sprays.

Naturally, there were exceptions to this restraint. 80 On a salver made by Edward Capper in 1772 a coat-of-arms occurs within a border of classical urns and profiles which are individual enough to suggest that they may have been portraits of the members of the family for whom the salver was made. Here Neo-classical decoration is shown at its most exuberant.

While classical ornament was predominant at this period, other styles occurred. Chinoiserie motifs were still acceptable, mostly in the form of engraved Chinese characters on tea caddies made by William Lutwyche

and John Vere, and others in the late 1760s. Gothic and 81 naturalistic motifs, though subdued, are also found. The former is featured in the pierced work on oval salt cellars and boat-shaped sweetmeat baskets, where the decoration often consists of simple arches or pales below Vitruvian scrolls.

Table silver, hitherto mostly variations of the heavy Hanoverian pattern, becomes light of aspect and light of grip in the Old English pattern. It has remained popular ever since. This was frequently decorated, with either bright-cutting, feathering or wrigglework. Irish spoons and forks are often bright-cut, but in a highly characteristic way. The terminal is usually ornamented with an oval cartouche composed of bright-cut strokes made to look like a sunburst. The Neo-classical dawn had reached even Dublin.

Small items, such as snuffboxes, vinaigrettes, patch-boxes, wine labels, sugar tongs and teaspoons, were 79

79 A group of wine labels. **a** Cider, flat-chased. Sandylands Drinkwater. London, about 1755. **b** Port, bright-cut. James Hyde. London, about 1790. **c** Madeira, bright-cut. John Sanders. London, 1807. **d** Burgundy, embossed. Margaret Binley. London, about 1770. **e** Claret, flat-chased. Unmarked, about 1760. **f** Bucellas, engraved and bright-cut. George Knight. London, 1824. **g** Lisbon, pierced and tooled. Hester Bateman. London, about 1770. **h** Port, flat-chased. Hester Bateman. London, about 1770. **i** Madeira. Thomas Phipps & Edward Robinson. London, 1779. Collection of Michael Parkington, Esq.

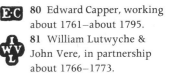

80 Edward Capper, working about 1761–about 1795.
81 William Lutwyche & John Vere, in partnership about 1766–1773.

produced in enormous quantities, and of sufficiently diverse and original designs for them to be easily collected today. Already the silver industry was extending to the novelty market, a trend which developed even further as silver bullion became cheaper in the 19th century.

Until 1773 silver produced in Sheffield and Birmingham had to go to Chester, York or Newcastle for assay, and on rarer occasions to London. On the round trip designs, especially those from Boulton & Fothergill's establishment, were pirated by less scrupulous firms, and breakages occurred. Consequently, largely due to the efforts of Matthew Boulton, Sheffield and Birmingham were allowed to open Assay Offices, the mark of the former being a crown, and the latter, an anchor. The committee involved in urging the foundation of the offices, it is said, met at an inn called the Crown and Anchor.

The magnificent, the mediocre and the trivial occur in late 18th-century silver. Industrial techniques changed the craft beyond the dreams of Paul de Lamerie, while individual designers and craftsmen looked for patronage to growing firms like Boulton & Fothergill, and Rundell, Bridge & Rundell or Wakelin & Garrard.

Altogether a thriving commercial climate and a manufacturing revolution combined with the company-mindedness of men like Boulton and the design talent of men like Adam and Flaxman to create a setting in which silver ceases to be an upper class indulgence and becomes a truly social art. It is in terms of the mass appeal of silver that the next generation of silversmiths had to work, and behind them the expanding retail goldsmiths and jewellers. From 1800 onwards silver can only be understood in terms of 'the lengthening shadow' of their influence.

Regency Silver

By the end of the 18th century the Adam style had been in fashion for about thirty years. Very little had escaped its influence. Debased and mass-produced, it had lost the freshness that the early work of Adam had possessed. The run of victories by Nelson and Wellington which effectively contained the Napoleonic expansion gave Britain a sense of her own power. In modest ways British liberal opinion was beginning to have material success—for example, the abolition of the slave trade in 1807. British supremacy in industry and on the ocean was creating that mentality which was to be the foundation of her imperial expansion. Indeed the early Victorians were very conscious of the formative years of the Regency period. This also applied to silver.

Not surprisingly, the idea grew that there was something fundamentally less than robust about a society which had to rely on the artefacts of another civilisation rather than on its own. On the other hand, the late 18th century had seen the rise of systematic historical study as we know it today. The historical approach to civilisation, together with the standard classical education and the never-ending Grand Tours, meant that the question of historical roots and contemporary achievements were interrelated. In design, therefore, the historicist approach persisted in the Regency period, but it also faced the problem of mechanical production. No longer was it sufficient to imitate a Greek cup; now it was necessary to create a cup which expressed the artistic legacy of antiquity as well as the natural fecundity of English minds and machines. Machine-digested styles had now to be as good as the best of the past, and as original as sensibility would allow. A sense of history was important. A sense of progress had to be encouraged. For this reason, Regency silver is complex. It is classical, eclectic, original and imaginative. It looks backwards to the time-tested models of Greece and Rome; it looks forward to the naturalism of the years before and after the Great Exhibition of 1851. This complexity was to be the basis of the evolution of a characteristically Victorian style in which designers sought to create a style as individual and historic in its own right as Queen Anne, Régence or Adam.

The Regency period, therefore, is of great importance in any understanding of later developments in English silver. During the years 1800–1820 a synthesis of traditionalism and technical achievement occurred which increasingly had to take stock of the vitality and importance of Romanticism.

The person chiefly responsible for outmoding the Adam style was Charles Heathcote Tatham (1772–1842), who worked under Henry Holland. Tatham travelled in Italy between 1794 and 1797, staying mostly in Rome and Naples, where he became friendly with Canova. In 1797 Tatham travelled back to England via Dresden, Berlin and Prague, making architectural drawings on the way. Subsequently, in 1799, he published *Ancient and Ornamental Architecture at Rome and in Italy*. In 1806 he published *Designs for Ornamental Plate*, in which he demanded massive effect as well as detailed and finely finished ornament. He was a leader of fashion, setting silversmiths a difficult task. Only a few makers, such as Paul Storr (who worked for Rundell, Bridge & Rundell from 1807 to 1819), and Benjamin Smith senior (who worked for Rundell's from 1802 to 1814, and later for Green, Ward & Green) could hope to achieve any degree of success.

Paradoxically it was Tatham's classical consciousness which was to demand an end to the trivialisation of classical styles. Classicism had to be not so much rejected as rethought. It was the stylistic anaemia of Adam that was called in question.

At first the battle to quench the Adam style was difficult. After all, it had become a habit with designers, manufacturers and the public alike. Tatham, however, had support from architects like Holland and James Wyatt who was later to go over to the Gothic style. More than by anyone else, he was encouraged by George IV, then Prince Regent, who eventually ordered much splendid plate in the grand manner. Soon the firm of Rundell, Bridge & Rundell was supplying a large amount of silver of this kind not only to the Crown, but also to most of the nobility, whose inclination it was to follow the Crown in matters of taste. Previously George III had shown little or no interest in silver. In part this explains the lethargy of the silver trade at the close of the 18th century.

Monumental pieces in the new style, basically for display in large houses, began to appear during the late 1790s. A tea urn of a similar date, by Paul Storr, displays the use of ancient motifs on a shape based on originals in marble or bronze. The scrolling snake handles, which were to reappear on tea services, cups and other articles for the next ten years, had been used on Adam silver of the 1770s and early 1780s. Along with the shallow curved flutes in bands, and the stiff palm-leafage at the base of the body, these suggest that Neo-classicism was being transformed more than rejected. Silver of a less ambitious nature also underwent a change. A coffee jug, made in 1805, for instance,

82 A George III coffee jug. William Burwash & Richard Sibley. London, 1810.

83 An early 19th-century American soup tureen. Simon Chaudron. Philadelphia, about 1813. New-York Historical Society, New York City.

84 A George III silver-gilt sideboard dish, chased with a fox-hunting scene. William Pitts. London, 1809.

85 Paul Storr, 1771–1844.

86 Benjamin Smith senior, working from about 1799, died 1823.

82

83

84

47

87 A large pair of George III winecoolers in
Louis XV style. Paul Storr for Rundell,
Bridge & Rundell. London, 1813.

shows a move away from the baluster- or vase-shape
of the previous decades towards something a little more
adventurous and interesting.

Designers were turning for inspiration not only to
Rome, but to other civilisations like that of Egypt.
Napoleon's illfated Middle East campaign had involved
archaeologists and surveyors who recovered the magic
of the Pyramid civilisation. Architects were quick to
adopt their findings. For example, an Egyptian Hall
was erected in Piccadilly in 1812 based on the Temple
of Tentyra described in 'Denon's celebrated work'.
As early as 1806 a six-light candelabrum in the Egyptian
style had been made by Benjamin Smith and his partner
89 Digby Scott. The branches spring from the heads of
three winged sphinx caryatids, while vulture motifs
appear on the triform base, a shape which incidentally
lingered until the Great Exhibition. Even earlier a silver-
gilt vase and cover decorated with anthemions and
sphinx-like monsters, from the collection of the Duke
of Bedford, and dating from 1800, should be mentioned.
Made by Paul Storr, it reflects the new awareness
engendered by Tatham's architectural approach. The
animal-leg supports are each headed by a winged
sphinx, and the body is applied with a grotesque
grinning mask below a border of exaggerated anthemion
motifs. The Graeco-Egyptian flavour of the piece was
no doubt inspired by Thomas Hope (about 1770–1831).
Hope, the virtuoso and author, made a large collection

of sculptures, was a patron of Canova, Thorwaldsen and
Flaxman, and published in 1807 *Household Furniture
and Interior Decoration.*

The flair with which such an imaginative design was
culled from original sources and contemporary research
reflects the trouble which for the most part the great
firm of Rundell, Bridge & Rundell took to please their
clients who were tired of Adam forms but excited by the
mystique of the empire of Cheops and Cleopatra.

In his essay 'A Problem of Artistic Responsibility'
Charles Oman writes: 'It was the aim of Rundell and
Bridge to remedy this by the establishment of a workshop which gave scope to craftsmen of the best ability
working from designs by first class artists who would be
liberally rewarded. This was clearly the brain-child
of John Bridge, who was applying to silver the technique so successfully used by Josiah Wedgwood in the
field of ceramics.' It was probably through John
Bridge (1755–1834), or at least a farmer-relative of his
who knew George III, that the firm was given the
standing of Jewellers, Gold- and Silversmiths to the
Crown, also obtaining similar warrants from the Prince
of Wales and the Duke of York.

The French Revolution played an important part in the
fortunes of Rundell and Bridge. Refugees escaping from
France brought jewellery and plate to Britain. Once
here, they naturally disposed of it through the Royal
Goldsmiths, and it is said that Philip Rundell (1743–

88 A George III hot-water jug. Digby Scott & Benjamin Smith senior. London, 1805. Victoria and Albert Museum, London.

 **89** Digby Scott & Benjamin Smith senior, in partnership 1802–1807.

90 A George III silver-gilt three-light centrepiece with alternative fittings. Possibly Philip Cornman. London, 1810.

1827) was able to acquire a large amount of French plate made by leading craftsmen of the 18th century. He seems also to have obtained much plate at an earlier period from the French owners who hoped to reclaim it after the Revolution.

Quite apart from providing Rundell's with the backing needed to finance their workshops and design department, this acquisition of French originals had an important effect on the firm's output. Rundell, seeing the work by French masters such as Thomas Germain (1674–1745) and his son François, Jacques Rottiers, and the Rococo work of the Meissonier school, no doubt was given plenty to think about. 'The renewal of the war with France in 1803 and the consequent advance of rents generally, from which the landed gentry profited,' says Penzer, 'produced a fresh outburst of extravagance, and orders for large services of plate and costly jewellery poured into Ludgate Hill', where Rundell's had their premises.

The revived Rococo style, which as we have seen was largely inspired by such French silver, was yet another source for a form of naturalistic design with a pedigree stretching back through Adam van Vianen and Renaissance art. On the other hand etchings and designs by artists like Jacques François Saly (1717–1776) and George Michael Moser (1704–1783) were also a mine of inspiration for the upsurge of Rococo effects in the Regency period. When simply copied, such effects were

no more successful than their counterparts had been seventy years earlier, though items like a massive pair of winecoolers by Storr (1813), probably taken from Louis XV originals, were executed with consummate skill. This style had its bitter critics, and rightly so. Given its Rundell patronage, however, it made it all too easy for mediocre craftsmen, and manufacturers like Gainsford & Nicholson of Sheffield, to turn out uninspired amalgams of Rococoesque objects. For all its shortcomings, it was the naturalism within these styles that was to prove the most productive and important. It was through the vagaries of naturalism that the art of the silversmith was to advance.

Rundell's continued to be the most important element in the revival of the silver business after 1800. In their heyday they employed not only the outstanding silversmiths Benjamin Smith and Paul Storr, but vast numbers of the best workmen, sculptors, modellers and designers. The best-known of their staff included William Theed, R.A. (1764–1817) who had also worked for Wedgwood and who was head of the design department at Rundell's until his death; the sculptor, John Flaxman (1755–1826); Thomas Stothard (1755–1834), the painter and book illustrator; and Edward Hodges Baily (1788–1867), Flaxman's pupil, who joined Rundell's in 1815 and was later to work for Paul Storr and John Mortimer.

The snake-head spout of a tea urn of 1816 in the Egyptian style by Digby Scott and Benjamin Smith bears a close resemblance to that on a kettle made by Paul Storr in 1802, and to a tea urn made by him in 1809. It is probable that the dies from which these workshops cast their silver were in fact the property of Rundell's. This would explain why the two different firms of Storr and Smith should produce identical items. The same applies to the Trafalgar Vase, made by Benjamin Smith in 1808, one of many Lloyd's Patriotic Fund Vases which these insurance brokers presented as rewards for valour in an attempt to boost the efforts of army and navy personnel at the height of the struggle with Napoleon. Designed by John Flaxman, these vases were made for Rundell's by both Benjamin Smith and Paul Storr.

Perhaps the most popular single subject for vases was the Warwick Vase. Recovered from a pool on the site of Hadrian's Villa, the original marble was purchased by the Earl of Warwick in 1774. Engravings of the piece by Piranesi were done in 1778, and others were published in 1800. By about 1812 the Royal Goldsmiths were producing soup tureens, winecoolers and presentation cups to the same design. The most important was a set of twelve made between 1812 and 1814 for the Prince Regent. Later it was widely adapted for other silver items. For example, the lion's pelt detail on the Warwick Vase reappears in 1812 in the form of a silver-gilt wine label.

Once dies were made they could be used in a variety of ways by a variety of silversmiths. No wonder such

87

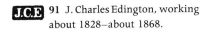 **91** J. Charles Edington, working about 1828–about 1868.

 92 Edward Cornelius Farrell, about 1775–1850.
93 Samuel Whitford senior, working about 1807–about 1830.
94 William Elliott, working about 1810–about 1843.

 95 John Emes, working from about 1796, died 1808.
96 Rebecca Emes & Edward Barnard, in partnership 1808–1828.
97 William Fountain, working about 1785–about 1805.

eminent firms as Hunt & Roskell (late Storr & Mortimer), G. R. Collis & Co. (formerly run by Edward Thomason), and R. & S. Garrard of Panton Street, Haymarket, London, were to buy heavily in the sale of Rundell's equipment when the firm closed in 1842. Through such dies and moulds Regency designs and brilliant details directly influenced silver in the mid Victorian period. Indeed manufacturers were to boast of the Rundell pedigree of their work.

In a firm like Rundell's the temptation was to reuse old designs and casts. Such was the tendency after Paul Storr left the firm in 1819, leaving the Dean Street workshops under the supervision of Cato Sharp (about 1772–1832). Rundell retired in 1823 (with a fortune amounting to about £1,500,000), but already the firm was losing its hold and little progress was made, especially after Bridge died in 1834. This great Regency firm, therefore, largely through the fixity of its own brilliance suffered an eclipse like that of Adam. Nevertheless, its tradition of informed styling, brilliant craftsmanship and adventurous spirit did not die altogether as can be seen in the rather experimental cup which Rundell's had had made for the Tzar as a presentation piece for Edward Thomason as late as 1830.

As time passed, the outlines of earlier classical shapes gradually softened in the work of both Storr and Smith by the introduction of less formal leafage. Later this tended to turn into scrolls. Line was also relieved by the use of sculptured figures or romanticised classical groups modelled in relief. Such features occur in a charger made by Storr in 1814, and on a centrepiece of 1816. The Theocritus Cup, designed by Flaxman sometime before 1811, is also an example of the trend which was to be influential. The campana (bell) shape of the body is relieved by groups of figures below vine tendrils which extend downwards, interlacing as handles above the spreading foot. Perhaps more than Flaxman, it was his pupil E. H. Baily who brought a new sculpturesque element to design. Indeed he is better known as a sculptor than a silver modeller. Having joined Rundell's in 1815, he was appointed chief modeller after Flaxman's death in 1826.

Rundell's were not the only retail goldsmiths, though their staff and international reputation and ability made them the most influential. Green, Ward & Green of Ludgate Street, and later of Cockspur Street, Pall Mall, were also a sizeable establishment. They supplied the Wellington Shield, designed by Thomas Stothard and made by Benjamin Smith, as well as the two gigantic candelabra, made in 1816 by Smith, which were presented to the Duke of Wellington by the merchants and bankers of the City of London. These pieces are now in Apsley House, London. Later Green's were supplied with **91** silver from the workshops of J. Charles Edington. Fisher, Braithwaite & Jones of the City, Kensington

Lewis of St James's, and David Ellis of Oxford Street were other, though much smaller, retail concerns.

Among the more ambitious of the working silversmiths of this period were Samuel Whitford, Edward Cornelius Farrell, William Pitts and William Elliott. These silversmiths specialised in articles which reflected the trend away from classical motifs and shapes. They mixed their designs with a degree of naturalism. Anthemion motifs expanded out of their original shapes into tendril-like scrolls which terminated in honeysuckle fronds. The vine-leaf, successfully used by Storr as controlled decoration, gradually gained importance. It is seen to effect in candlesticks of 1816 by Benjamin Smith. The bases are applied with modelled figures, but otherwise the whole design is swallowed in the meandering grape vine. A large silver-gilt tankard of 1816 by Edward C. Farrell, is equally applied with a border of **92** apples and grapes, while the barrel is decorated with naturalistic figures. They owe their style more to 17th-century German ivory and silver tankards than to anything from Greece or Rome, although the scene depicted is a classical one. Farrell's preoccupation with this kind of subject is even better examplified in a tea kettle of 1822. The basic shape is of a mid 18th-century English origin, while the cast and applied figures are taken from the 17th-century paintings of Teniers. A silver-gilt dish of 1824, also by Farrell, has a wide chased border of Stuart flowers and leaves found on porringers and dishes of the 1670s. In candlesticks of 1819 Samuel Whitford shows a complete disregard for proportion in **93** an effort, one supposes, to eliminate the prevailing classicism. He portrays Oriental gentlemen in a rustic manner, each holding a candle sconce shaped like an overgrown bloom. William Elliott, however, who used a **94** similar theme in 1818, produced better results.

All these items display the highest craftsmanship, but they remain overgrown classical pieces rather than new productions. To Flaxman's designs are added naturalistic free-modelled details which developed into the various forms of naturalism in the silver of the 1830s and 1840s. Paul Storr's hive-shaped honeypots and barrel-shaped teapots of the 1790s had been adventurous, but these were exceptions rather than the rule.

Other good London makers of the period include John Emes, who died in 1808 when the business was carried **95** on by his widow Rebecca. Mrs Emes was soon joined in partnership by her husband's workshop manager Edward Barnard, founder of the large manufacturing **96** concern. John Emes specialised in a fine quality, though usually less ambitious form of the classical style. His oval butter dishes feature pierced borders of formal scrolling leafage which was often found in a bolder form on plate from Rundell's. William Fountain was another **97** silversmith of repute whose training in the Adam style mixed uneasily with the new romantic vision. The old-

100 established firm of Hennell (founded in 1736) continued to manufacture well made articles, as well as those which almost totally lack imagination. R. & S. Garrard was another well known firm whose business connexions extended back through Edward Wakelin to George Wickes in the 1720s. As time went on they began to rise in importance until by the 1820s they were second only to Rundell's. By then the latter were fast declining in importance. Garrard's eventually became the Royal Goldsmiths in 1840 and have remained so ever since.

120
101 The silver-gilt Thomason Cup of 1830, bearing the mark of John Bridge, is yet another example of the Romantic expression from Rundell's workshop. A bell-shaped bowl rises from an applied calyx of thorny leafage and poppies on a similarly decorated stem. Reminiscent of Gothic architecture and ironwork, it is a successful design, which shows how Rococo forms, heightened naturalism and the newly fashionable Gothic could be combined. A. W. N. Pugin (1812–1852) was found at the age of fifteen sketching in the Print Room at the British Museum by one of the staff at Rundell's. He was invited to execute various Gothic designs for them, some of which survive at the Victoria and Albert Museum. Thus the Gothic movement, which

continued alongside the Rococo for the next twenty years, was also encouraged by Rundell's. As Shirley Bury's articles 'The Lengthening Shadow of Rundell's' show, they were almost directly responsible for shaping the designs and general trends of silver for the remainder of the century.

Ordinary domestic silver prolonged rather than challenged the styles of the late 18th century. This applies particularly to tea and coffee sets, candlesticks, cups, salvers, table silver and salt cellars. As time progressed the simpler styles of these items gradually took on the general outlines and shapes of the grander, more experimental articles. Tea and coffee sets were oblong. Soon they assumed a softer central horizontal line through the introduction of a moulded, applied or engraved girdle. Milk jugs, formerly of a tapering vase-shape with high loop handles and square pedestal bases, became straighter at the sides. As with the more expensive silver, articles of a thinner gauge became more and more decorated. Especially in Birmingham and Sheffield, embossed scrolls, foliage, flutes and flowers could be produced cheaply by the steam presses. Early examples of this style, in both silver and Sheffield plate, began to appear around 1800. Thomas Nicholson (1799–1860), of

99 A George III silver-gilt bachelor's teapot. John Emes. London, 1806.

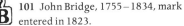 100 Robert, David & Samuel Hennell, mark entered in 1802.

 101 John Bridge, 1755–1834, mark entered in 1823.

the Sheffield firm Gainsford & Nicholson, claimed to have introduced the shells and dolphins into gadroon mounts because, it was said, everyone was becoming weary of the plain designs in silver wares. Later he also claimed to have introduced the arabesques and strapwork found on so much plate of the 1840s and 1850s. It was quite obvious to Nicholson, as well as to designers like Tatham and Stothard, that the time was well overdue for a complete reappraisal of design.

By about 1815 both the English Regency of Rundell's and also the French Empire styles had much impressed American silversmiths. These men in their turn were rebelling against Adamesque effects, bringing their gifts of reinterpretation into play, and sometimes producing highly individualistic items. In Philadelphia particularly, owing to the influence of the French immigrants Simon Chaudron and Anthony Rasch, silversmiths were keen to produce articles in an often massive Neo-classical style. Chaudron, for instance, manufactured an impressive soup tureen (about 1813) for presentation to Captain Jacob Jones. Now in the collection of the New York Historical Society, this piece is in the form of a low urn supported on a shaped pedestal base. The body is embellished with acanthus-leafage below classical medal-

lions, and either side is applied with a mask and leaf handle. The cover is surmounted by a seated allegorical figure. Harvey Lewis and Thomas Fletcher, also of Philadelphia, worked in this style. Indeed, the latter, who had made several trips to London, is said to have produced work equal to that of Benjamin Smith or Paul Storr. In fact Thomas Fletcher and his partner Sidney Gardiner were well known for their elaborate presentation pieces. In this respect their efforts to reward American heroes of the 1812 War matched the English concern which had created the Lloyd's Patriotic Fund Vases or the Duke of Wellington's candelabra.

Obadiah Rich of Boston was another early 19th-century American silversmith of considerable talent. An inkwell which he made about 1830, believed to have been designed by the sculptor Horatio Greenough, and now in the Fogg Art Museum, Harvard University, features a central urn upheld by three reeded supports each terminating in a hound's head. This piece, while of great merit, is only another expression of the longing for Regency grandeur. American silver, however, had to wait for the experimental forces engendered in the 1870s by Tiffany & Co. of New York for a more truly national style.

On a more domestic level American silversmiths of the

83

53

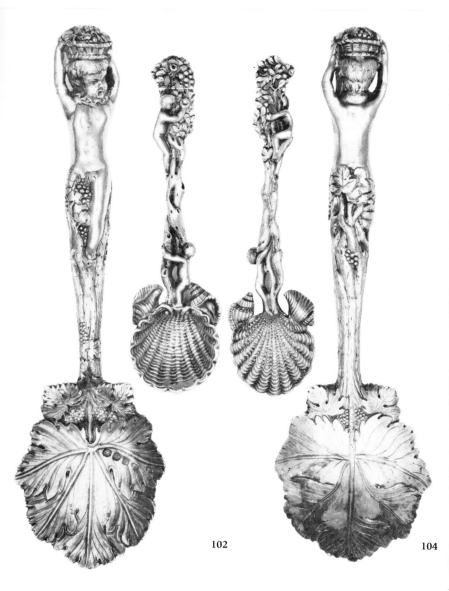

102 Four silver-gilt decorative spoons. Edward Cornelius Farrell. London, 1818–1824.

103 A pair of George III silver-gilt tapersticks. William Elliott. London, 1818.

102

104

103

104 A George III tea set. Paul Storr for
Rundell, Bridge & Rundell. London, 1815.

107 John Harvey, working about 1739–about 1750.

108 Sandylands Drinkwater, working about 1731–1772.

109 Thomas Phipps & Edward Robinson, working until about 1820, firm's mark entered about 1784.

a   b   c

d   e   f

g   h   i

1820s and 1830s managed to combine classical shapes with the melon forms then popular in London. William Thompson, John Targee, John W. Forbes and Garret Eoff, all leading craftsmen of New York, continued to supply tea sets and other utilitarian pieces. Often decorated with broad lobes, American work of the period also featured stamped borders in the Franco-Dutch manner, incorporating wheat-sheaves and patriotic emblems. With the introduction of these and other chased decorations American silver increasingly reflected the ideals of English manufacturers such as Thomas Nicholson of Sheffield.

During the period 1770–1800, the wine label had emerged in England with a greater variety of designs. **107,108** Makers like John Harvey and Sandylands Drinkwater had been the first to produce them in the 1730s and 1740s. Their designs were either a variation of the escutcheon, plain or flat-chased with vines and bunches of grapes, or a cast and chased arrangement of scrolls. Leaves, cherubs

and bearded masks in the Rococo tradition were also popular. Gradually more makers began to specialise in these decorative and collectable items. Makers of the 18th century who excelled in the design and execution of wine labels were Phipps & Robinson, Margaret Binley, **109,1** Thomas Howell, Bateman & Co., and James Hyde. **111,1** Matthew Boulton, the Birmingham manufacturer, also made some interesting examples in the Adam style. By 1755 the design of wine labels had been considerably **79** diversified. The most common are the 'Crescent' (either plain, with beaded borders, pierced, or embellished with bright-cut decoration or engraving); the 'Navette' (a roughly eye-shaped oval); 'Rectangular' (with plain or reeded borders and cut corners); 'Scroll' (usually plain, with feathered or bright-cut borders, but sometimes surmounted by an oval or shield for crest or initials); and the 'Goblet' (plain or festooned). From about 1800 **105** onwards, however, patterns for wine labels underwent a change, and nowhere more than in the respective work-

105 A group of wine labels. **a** Sherry, cast and chased. Charles Rawlings & William Summers. London, 1855. **b** Port, cast and chased. Rawlings & Summers. London, 1846. **c** Madeira, cut and chased. John Edward Terrey & Co. London, 1828. **d** Claret, cast, pierced and chased. Edward Cornelius Farrell. London, 1817. **e** Sherry, cast, chased and silver-gilt. Paul Storr for Rundell, Bridge & Rundell. London, 1811. Based on a detail from the Warwick Vase. **f** Burgundy, cast, chased and silver-gilt. Philip Rundell. London, 1820. **g** I. (for 'Irish') Whiskey, cast and chased. Charles Reily & George Storer. London, 1833. **h** Madeira, cast and chased. Rebecca Emes & Edward Barnard. London, 1823.

i Champagne, cast, pierced and chased. Thomas Phipps & Edward Robinson. London, 1817. Collection of Michael Parkington, Esq.

106 A George IV teapot. Robert Gainsford. Sheffield, 1820. A machine-made piece, displaying the worst features of design poorly adapted to mass-production.

shops of Storr and of Smith. Rundell's succeeded in promoting an interest in these labels which were shown to great effect on the glass decanters, both coloured and clear, that were then fashionable. That such a small item as the wine label should attract the attention of so great a firm points to their attention to detail. In the great houses the wine label was an important acquisition. Storr produced some stunning examples, as did Benjamin Smith. Usually heavily cast and chased, patterns included bold scallop-shells, revivals of the John Harvey grape-and-cherub theme, and massive quatrefoils. Other firms experimented with these small designs, notably Reily & Storer, Emes & Barnard, Rawlings & Summers, John E. Terrey & Co., Edward C. Farrell, R. & S. Garrard and Hunt & Roskell. Most of these firms produced many interesting examples well into the 1860s. Good specimens of a later date are rare, for wine labels were increasingly made redundant by the introduction of paper labels.

The first quarter of the 19th century marked a period of transition in the silver industry. Cheap labour, growing wealth, the expansion of firms like Rundell's, as well as peace after a long costly war, had their effect. Large London firms were obliged to make every effort to revive a market tired of Adam. They also had to compete with their rivals in Sheffield and Birmingham. Mass-production methods, however sophisticated, did not automatically promote fine quality. Tribute must be paid to Rundell's who through experiment, research and design, as well as an eye for the best artists and craftsmen of the day, were able to raise the craft out of the Adam-esque mire on to a plateau of excellence. During the Regency period the seeds of naturalism were sown. An artistic climate was created in which the next generation of designers and critics could take deeper stock of the question of design in general and of silver design in particular.

3,114
115

Early Victorian Silver

In *Ancient and Ornamental Architecture at Rome and in Italy* Charles Heathcote Tatham had written: 'The works of the Ancients are a MAP TO THE STUDY OF NATURE they teach us what objects we are to select for imitation and the method in which they may be combined for effect.' Editions of this work appeared in 1799, 1810, 1826 and 1843. The phrases 'select for imitation' and 'combined for effect' provide us with the keys to an understanding of silver in the period 1820–1850. Throughout these years designers were either selecting antique models which could be adapted for modern purposes or they were selecting natural objects either from 18th-century originals or from nature itself. These they imitated, using the precision methods of electro-typing and other reproduction techniques. In passing they tried to give these products some sort of usefulness.

On the other hand classical models and nature were rich sources of decoration. Not content with imitation, the early Victorians in an attempt to emulate French excellence in design began to 'combine for effect'. To them it was the most proper thing in the world to combine elements from all these sources, their brilliant imitation of them being beyond criticism. It was thought that the excellence of the parts would guarantee the artistic excellence of the whole.

It was left to the art critics and the art periodicals to show that 'combinations' needed to be as judiciously selected as items for imitation. In the publications of the 1840s and 1850s the naivety of eclecticism was to be exposed, while leaving intact the sense of progress that had been made in the arts and industry. The art periodicals were concerned with the close ties which they rightly saw must exist between design and production in a technological society. In every issue the practical merits of design-consciousness are again and again hammered out in theory. If only manufacturers and the public alike could be educated into thinking seriously about design, they write, then thousands of objects would indeed be well made, useful and beautiful in an original way. This was the mentality behind the exhibitions in Manchester in 1845–1846 and Birmingham in 1848, and their success encouraged Henry Cole and Prince Albert to plan the Great Exhibition of 1851.

In the middle years of the 19th century, silver was bought by large sections of the public. In order to put their goods within the reach of everybody, silver manufacturers were price-conscious. Catalogues generally showed two types of silver. These were the expensive display pieces such as cups and centrepieces, which were the *sine qua non* of public presentations, and household articles like coffee pots and table silver. The latter could be divided into the better quality and the mass-produced either in silver, Sheffield plate or electroplate. British silver also had an international market. Even Rundell's had had agents in St Petersburg and Rio de Janeiro. Competition was keen between the leading manufacturers and between them and the French silversmiths. Joseph Angell's publicity pamphlet (1851) reads: 'Joseph Angell ... trusts he may be excused possessing a portion of that spirit of commercial enterprise which has stimulated so much exertion in this modern field of competition ... ' British pre-eminence in price, solidity and workmanship was claimed, and the pamphlet goes on: 'to produce ... articles of utility at a cost placing them within the reach of all, should be the aim and object of every manufacturer.'

Silver consciously reflected Britain's sense of Empire. A large shield representing 'Britannia welcoming the Nations of the Earth, and extending her hand of succour to Africa, as raising her from her degraded position' was typical of the period. The allegorical figures of the four principal rivers of the world puts the Thames on a par with the Mississippi, the Nile and the Indus.

In 1845–1846 and 1848 exhibitions were held, leading up to the Great Exhibition of 1851. These 'set at rest fears that foreign ingenuity could surpass our national pre-eminence in these manufactures'. An emphasis was placed on technical mastery, and brilliance of manufacture was seen as the equivalent of 'British'. Manufacturers, however, were conscious of the merit of French designs, and firms like Hunt & Roskell and Elkington's were not slow to employ the Frenchmen Antoine Vechte (1799–1868), Pierre-Emile Jeannest (1813–1857) and later Léonard Morel-Ladeuil (1820–1888).

Silver was judged by its originality. The Goldsmiths' Company of London awarded their prizes on this principle at the Great Exhibition. According to the *Morning Chronicle,* it was Garrard's who had the largest number of original designs on show. Originality in fact meant original combinations of revered styles. In this there was a good deal of confusion: a tea caddy or casket which had a medallion of Anthony and Cleopatra and another of Love and War was considered 'from the antique', as though classical themes were thought to be enough to make the object classical. It cost £41.

At the Great Exhibition a chased 'Tea and Coffee Equipage, in frosted silver, relieved with turquoise ENAMEL' was shown. Its maker, Joseph Angell, claimed the first introduction of enamel into this type of article.

116 An early Victorian silver-gilt dessert
stand and cover. R. & S. Garrard & Co.
London, 1839.

 117 Joseph Angell junior, about
1816–1891, mark entered in 1849.
118 Robert Garrard, in overall
control of firm by 1802, this mark
entered in 1827.

119 A George IV four-light candelabrum. Rebecca Emes & Edward Barnard. London, 1828. This eclectic design, featuring both Gothic and Greek motifs, was in part based on a 'Drawg. from an old Engrav. of an ancient fragment in India'. According to the makers' account, it was originally supplied to the retail silversmith David Ellis, of John Street, London, at a cost of £183 7s. 6d.

Manufacturers rivalled each other in making such technological progress and adding such colourful details. By these means they tried to outdo the precision of electroplated goods. A note adds, 'It is easily cleaned'. The question of utility was slowly being raised.

The Victorians set great store by education and moral improvement. Children's mugs were chased with appropriate scenes from Defoe's *Robinson Crusoe*. In essence it was a practical morality. Their belief was in the 'greatest happiness for the greatest numbers', and the growth of mass-production which created benefits for everyone. The mass-production of silver was a moral achievement. Possession of silver was a sign not only of prosperity, but of cultural progress. Silver expressed a sense of improvement in the quality of life. That perhaps was one of the reasons for its popularity.

About 1800 Alessandro Volta invented the electric battery. As early as 1805 L. V. Brugnatelli had gilded medals by means of electrolysis, but his techniques were imperfect. In 1814 Paul Storr made a small silver-gilt goblet commissioned by Rundell's using an early form of electrogilding. This is indicative of the experimental outlook of Rundell, Bridge & Rundell. This 'Galvanic Goblet' was designed by John Flaxman. The work of Michael Faraday in 1821 prepared the way for the tests of J. F. Daniell, H. H. von Jacobi and Thomas Spencer. By the late 1830s Spencer could reveal the details of his electrodeposition techniques to the Liverpool Polytechnic Society. It was Elkington's of Birmingham, however, who patented the process using improved batteries which gave a continuous flow of electricity to produce firm deposits of metal from solutions of cyanides of gold and silver in cyanide of potassium. By 1841 Alexander Parkes, one of the firm's metallurgists, patented a process making electrotypes from nonmetallic moulds. In 1845 Elkington's bought a patent for a plating dynamo, which had been invented by J. S. Woolrich in 1842. Again in 1847 another employee, William Millward, invented the technique of bright-deposition, which made the burnishing of electroplated items largely unnecessary. By acquiring such patents Elkington's gained effective control of the electroplating industry which by 1855 had spread throughout England, virtually eclipsing Sheffield plate.

The results of this new process were revolutionary. By using unvulcanised rubber moulds into which a wax mixed with a conductive material was poured, copies of all sorts of natural objects like flowers were made in copper and then electroplated. Even antique silver could be exactly copied in the finest detail in silver or copper. No longer was there a gap between silver and plated articles. Parallel to developments in photography, electroplating was to fascinate people by the exactness of its processes. The popularity of detailed naturalism in silver and plated items in the middle years of the century policy of buying up new patents. They employed a huge staff, including some of the best designers and craftsmen of the day.

Other provincial manufacturers included Henry Wilkinson & Co. (Sheffield); Robinson, Edkins & Aston (Birmingham), the successors to the Matthew Boulton & Plate Co.; Ledsham, Vale & Wheeler (Birmingham); and Edward Thomason (Birmingham), who had been apprenticed to Matthew Boulton. Thomason's ambition was to win from Rundell's commissions for work for the Crown. This he never achieved. He died in 1849, having been knighted in 1832. His firm was later known as G. R. Collis & Co. Other large provincial firms included S. C. Younge & Co. (Sheffield); Marshall & Son (Edinburgh) T., J. & N. Creswick (Sheffield); James Dixon & Sons (Sheffield); and Thomas Bradbury & Sons (Sheffield).

Around the beginning of the 1820s the gauge of silver used in ordinary domestic ware began to thicken. After the Napoleonic Wars the country's economy grew stronger. New styles necessitated the use of heavier silver. Garrard's encouraged a style of 'traditional' naturalism in the 1820s and 1830s. Large melon forms, either ribbed or plain, were soon adapted by other manufacturers to their own designs for teapots and soup tureens, salt cellars and cups. Shapes and decorative details became less restrained, and the revival Rococo styles were further applied with drooping borders of lily blooms, vine-leaves and arabesques. In its weight and gauge, Victorian silver stands in contrast to that of the Adam period.

From the beginning of Victoria's reign manufacturers were encouraged seriously to consider design. French competition was growing, and it was obvious that the long tradition of schools for design set up by the French state were successful. By 1843 the Society of Arts, which had been founded in 1754, had its concern for manufacture and design revived under the presidency of Prince Albert. It proposed a series of industrial exhibitions. In France many such *expositions* had occurred since 1798. Firms were often afraid, however, that exhibitions would make design piracy easier. *The Art Journal* tried to counteract such fears, pointing out that a design registration Act had been passed in 1842. In 1847 Henry Cole (1808–1882), who had joined the Society in 1846, set up the 'Felix Summerly's Art Manufactures'. Its intention was to 'preserve the good old practice of connecting the best art with familiar objects of everyday use'. Cole invited various artists to assist in the project, notably the sculptor John Bell (1811–1895), the carver and designer W. Harry Rogers and the painter Richard Redgrave (1804–1888). Manufacturers of silver and plated goods involved included the Sheffield firms of Broadhead & Atkin, James Dixon & Son and Joseph Rogers & Son, and the London firm headed by Benjamin Smith junior (died 1850).

In 1848 *The Art-Union* still recommended the use of

was the product of amazement as much as taste. Silversmiths had to live up to the standards of imitation that electrolysis set. Accordingly every technique of enamelling, colouring, texturing and detailing were eagerly sought to add brilliance to their designs. The outcome was the overdecoration found in many items of plate shown at the Great Exhibition. There was an obsession with detail, while the question of proportion and function were overlooked.

Not only were new alloys like 'German' (nickel) and 'Argentine' silver discovered, but the technique of spinning the metals was extended by the application of steam power to the lathes. The metal was forced round a wooden form which was revolved at high speed so that the silver assumed its shape. Jugs and pots of all kinds, as well as covers and nozzles, bases and spouts, were produced by this technique. In the case of larger items, they were made in sections and then soldered together. Spinning was also suitable for the new Britannia metal which was a soft mixture of tin, copper and antimony. From about 1790 this had been the poor man's alternative to Sheffield plate and silver itself.

While Rundell's declined, other firms, probably supplemented with craft knowledge obtained through Rundell's, came to the fore. R. & S. Garrard, Edward Barnard & Sons and Storr & Mortimer (subsequently Hunt & Roskell) between them probably account for the finest English silver made at this period. As we have seen, Elkington & Co. of Birmingham was another large concern, gaining importance largely through their

125 Robinson, Edkins & Aston, successors to the Matthew Boulton & Plate Co., working late 1830s and 1840s.

 126 Ledsham, Vale & Wheeler, working 1820s and 1830s.

127 S. C. Younge & Co., working until about 1830, firm's mark entered in 1811.

128 Thomas, James & Nathaniel Creswick, working from about 1811.

129 James Dixon & Sons, working from about 1829.

130 Thomas Bradbury & Sons, working from about 1795, being successors to Fenton & Co.

131 Benjamin Smith junior, working from about 1816, died 1850.

naturalism to symbolise the object decorated. Fish servers were decorated with fish. Caddy spoons had handles formed as tea-plants. The periodical goes on: 'In the present day refined taste demands that there shall be that union of subject and ornament in which one shall not predominate to the detriment of the other.' In its use and application decoration should 'tell a story', and if 'Italian feeling' were needed, then by all means it should be evoked. This concept of design asked for moderation, but by 1852 even its basic concepts were being challenged by those who were not affronted by 'the barrenness of simple forms'. A telling aside, however, is found in the same periodical's comment on a design for a salt cellar by P.-E. Jeannest, the Frenchman who worked for Mintons of Stoke-on-Trent before joining Elkington's in 1849–1850. Its design, incorporating a young triton, a shell, seaweed and a dolphin, embodied the features it recommended. However, the periodical was to conclude: 'The designs of this artist will be found highly *suggestive* to the British manufacturer, although usually of a character too pronouncedly French for entire adoption.' Design was still affected by jealousy. English eclecticism, it seems, had to be entirely English. In 1849 *The Art Journal* reviewed Elkington's work for the Birmingham Exhibition. It noted that in the 'silver fabrications of these gentlemen, Art is progressing satisfactorily . . . The principal works executed . . . consist either of immediate adaptations of nature, or of close studies from the antique . . .' A dessert dish in the form of a tiger-lily was considered 'as graceful an object for the dinner table as can well be devised; and it is so because the artist has copied nature . . .' *The Art Journal* required artists 'to appeal to Nature for something more than bare imitations – we mean for ideas to be acted upon and carried out imaginatively.' As it was, nature was easier to imitate than to transform.

119 A candelabrum made by Emes & Barnard (1828) shows how successful an eclectic approach could be. Made in the form of a substantial column rising from a square base to four curved light-branches, it grows up towards a finely worked finial of leafage. The column is both square and faceted, and is chased with a variety of motifs ranging from bold anthemions to Gothic ruffles and fleurs-de-lys. To help us understand the confusion of such a design, we are fortunate in having the manufacturers' own account. This states that the design, incorporating as it does both Greek and Gothic ornaments, was also based on a 'Drawg. from an old Engrav. of an ancient fragment in India . . .' The piece is highly successful, in both design and execution.

The moral symbolism which Rundell's had pioneered was approved of by the artists. Classical themes were given a realistic treatment and applied to many of the enormous presentation pieces that were being produced. Grocers and Prime Ministers alike could expect some

122

form of testimonial at this period. A centrepiece given to William Ludlow of the Liverpool Philharmonic Society in 1846 figures Apollo playing a lyre, an Indian and a Philosopher, all on a scrolled pedestal. *The Art-Union* notes how this exhibits 'the influence of music alike on the savage and enlightened mind', and concludes that the design is 'admirably APPROPRIATE'. Of another piece in which Winter is represented by an old man 'shivering with cold, and warming his hands on a scant fire,' *The Art-Union* says: 'This is a well conceived idea worked out with infinite taste; the composition is instantly read . . . it is characterized by that graceful yet forcible simplicity which most deeply impresses the remembrance in works of Art.'

On the whole the 1840s disliked the notion of restraint. 'There would be but little room for improvement if the limits between which forms could be recognised as symmetrical had been rigidly defined. Just as natural forms of shells and flowers are rather suggestive than imperative to the artist, the few laws which mathematical forms impose are guides to taste rather than fetters on the exercise of its discretion.' It was in terms of this liberty that *The Art-Union* could applaud the eclectic work of Elkington's. It seemed more original than imitative of other styles. Indeed the art critics 'presumed to guard the manufacturer against the false taste that results from a profuse resort to the style known as that of Louis Quatorze'. Designers were warned against filling up 'an angle or square with two or three large scrolls', throwing in 'a few unnatural flowers', and

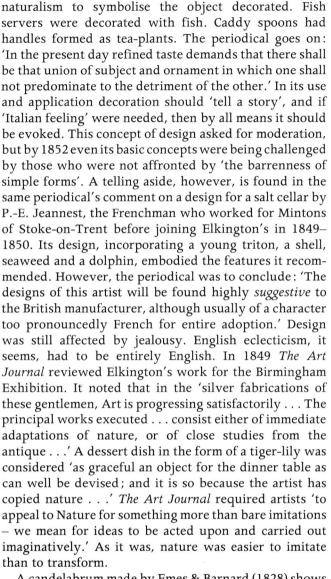

132 A William IV fish slice. Paul Storr of Storr & Mortimer. London, 1831.

133 An early Victorian presentation snuffbox. Elkington & Co. Birmingham, 1848. The gift of commercial travellers to Richard Cobden, M.P. (1804–1865), for his 'admirable and unwearied exertions in promoting the cause of Free Trade' (*Illustrated London News*).

N·M 134 Nathaniel Mills & Sons, working about 1826–about 1860.

E·S 135 Edward Smith, working during the 1830s and 1840s.

T&P 136 Taylor & Perry, working during the 1820s and 1830s.

C·F·H 137 Charles Frederick Hancock, about 1808–after 1870.

hoping that the article would 'pass current as old French'. Victorian Rococo was indeed a confusion of Régence, Rococo and naturalistic elements. Rococo shapes are often found in teapots and jugs of the period. Their oval forms and melon-shapes were carried over from the styles of the 1820s. By 1840 pear-shaped bodies were common. These were often decorated with genre subjects, like carousing peasants or scenes from Aesop's *Fables*. Copied by various manufacturers and shown at the Great Exhibition, these designs, further decorated with flowers, Rococo scrolls and shells, lasted well into the 1880s. Their earliest exponents had been Edward C. Farrell and William Elliott.

These Rococo shapes were, of course, modified by the addition of entwining foliage. Often the handles looked like perfectly formed plants. After 1845 the bodies of teapots and coffee pots were almost totally covered with naturalistic detail, and occasionally with engraved Chinoiserie, Gothic or arabesque features. The Farrell manner was continued in the productions of Barnard & Sons, Roberts & Hall, Henry Wilkinson & Co. and others. Many of the designs were patented under the Design Copyright Act, so there were few stylistic changes. If nothing else, however, the exaggerated designs reveal a restless search to find, if not 'something new' at least 'something original *and* sincere'.

In the late 1830s there was an upsurge in concern for design in relation to manufactured items as well as art objects. In 1839 the periodical *The Art-Union* appeared. Later, as *The Art Journal*, its circulation rose from 1,000 to 15,000, indicative of the substantial interest being shown in design. Its basic philosophy was that 'the greatest painters like Raphael did not disdain to become designers for the workers of the loom'. This in fact put into words the motto of Boulton and Wedgwood and Rundell, who had been most effectively aided by Fuseli, Adam and both the Flaxmans. *The Art Journal* tried to make design intelligible to manufacturers who readily adopted models which were foreign to the item produced. The appropriateness of a design was not only symptomatic of intellectual strength, but positively seen as a moral concern, even as an education. In the words of *The Art-Union* for 1st March 1848, artists were 'partners in educating the people; in improving the tastes, and consequently, the morals, of the community; in developing the intellectual strength and the intellectual resources of the United Empire'.

By 1851 the 'Felix Summerly's Art Manufactures' scheme, *The Art Journal* and the newly established art schools were bearing fruit. At least they were creating a more discriminating public which could see behind the elegance and prettiness of objects, including candlesticks or claret jugs, to a fundamental failure of design. The indiscriminate use of 'compounds of uncomfortable conventional shell-work' was seen as 'a brilliant piece of tastelessness', to quote the *Journal of Design and Manufactures* (1851). The glitter of material and over-elaborate manipulation of silver had its critics. Manufacture 'without one grain of thought or knowledge' was under attack.

The less successful designs of this period come from the workshops of Birmingham and Sheffield, either through a need for economy (dies, moulds and equipment were expensive), or a basic lack of design knowledge. Either way, there was a deterioration in design which was connected with the growing market. Nevertheless, firms of the calibre of Elkington's were to show how good design paid off even in mass-production. The novelty market, mostly confined to Birmingham, continued to produce a wide range of articles from butterfly-shaped chamber candlesticks by Ledsham, Vale & Wheeler to vinaigrettes and decorated snuffboxes by Nathaniel Mills & Sons, Edward Smith or Taylor & Perry. 134 135,136

By 1852, more as a reaction against the Great Exhibition than as a product of it, the *Journal of Design and Manufactures* raised the question, 'Which Direction is Ornamental Art likely to take?' 'Towards simplicity' was the answer. Aware that the concern for design had risen fifteen years before, it nevertheless rejected the idea that it was important that a piece of silver should be primarily 'Rococo', 'Louis Quatorze', 'Elizabethan' etc. It also rejected the form of naturalism which let coal scuttles and pianos 'tell their own story'. The vitality of naturalism was acknowledged in that the nature of an object and its function was sought rather than 'mere multitude and confusion of parts'. Already the conceptual seeds were being sewn for the advent of Christopher Dresser twenty years later.

With the Great Exhibition and the elaborate work of Garrard's, Hunt & Roskell, Smith & Nicholson and C. F. Hancock on the one hand, and the thoughtful criticisms 137 of the art periodicals on the other, silver design was subjected to discussion and public scrutiny. Silver manufacturers were again having to decide whether to produce what passed as 'art' or opt for the more difficult task of coping with the genuine problems of design.

The fascination of being able to reproduce exact copies of everything from a Roman cup to a flower slowed down the evolution of styles. For the moment it was enough to copy the achievements of previous silversmiths and to add naturalistic details to them. The Regency style was increasingly modified by this naturalism, although firms like G. R. Collis & Co. continued to make straightforward copies of Regency silver. Even Paul Storr worked in or reused ideas from this style until his retirement in 1839.

The vine- and acanthus-leaves and the classical ornaments of Regency designs were increasingly supplanted or modified by a naturalistic treatment. A cup, basically of classical shape, could now be decorated with irregular leafage rather than the symmetrical classical

138 *left* A George IV salt cellar, cast and
chased in the form of a sea-urchin. John Bridge
for Rundell, Bridge & Rundell. London, 1825.
right An early Victorian taperstick in the form
of a hare-bell. Edward Barnard & Sons. London,
1840. Victoria and Albert Museum, London.

138

motifs. From the 1830s this naturalistic trend gained momentum, aided by the Rococo designs which Rundell, Bridge & Rundell and Storr & Mortimer had popularised. It was thought artistic to add a classically modelled figure to a Rococo base. The figure would hold a basket or branches covered in realistic vine-leaves which would cluster into candleholders. To the base might be added dolphins. Such eclecticism, which imitated old styles and nature alike, was original only in its composition.

As early as the 1840s, however, items like a hare-bell taperstick were produced in which natural objects are not simply imitated, but transformed into something new. A natural shape is adapted, not as a piece of decoration, but to present the object itself in a startlingly original way. This natural transformation in no way disturbs the object's utility, but is integrated with it.

The naturalism in which the decoration swallowed the form of the piece had first appeared in the experimental work from Rundell's. For instance, a salt cellar of the 1820s appears as a sea-urchin resting on a base of coral. Based on the work of Nicholas Sprimont and other 18th-century exponents of Rococo naturalism, these pieces were attempts to transform the decoration into

a complete object so anticipating the full realised naturalism of the 1840s.

This form of naturalism was quite different from that which simply added vine-leaves to spherical teapots or smothered a cup in ivy. Naturalism, formerly just a design element, was to be the basis of a genuine advance in design. It raised the question of how man could best adapt natural objects and features to produce new things. Shapes were to be considered not as decorative additions, but as the essence of utility. Though such original pieces as the hare-bell taperstick 138 are rare, it does prove that silver in the naturalistic style of the 1830s and 1840s contained the idea that there was beauty in the way nature could be harnessed productively. Beauty was design. No extraneous pretty details were needed. Although Henry Cole and his associates were advocating these principles, their ideas were not taken up for another fifty years or more. As patternbooks such as Knight's *Vases and Ornaments* of 1833 show, art was equated with elaboration and imitation. It was a question of a mass-education in taste, *The Art Journal* declared. The fault, however, lay not only with the public, but with most of the manu-

139 *left* A William IV covered vase with cast and chased decoration. Charles Fox. London, 1833. Collection of Michael Parkington, Esq. *right* A William IV salver with engraved, flat-chased and cast decoration. William Bateman junior, one of Rundell, Bridge & Rundell's outworkers. London, 1835. Collection of Henry Walden, Esq.

140 *left* A William IV taperstick. Joseph Willmore. Birmingham, 1836. *centre* A William IV parcel-gilt inkstand. Walter Jordan. London, 1836. Collection of Sebastian Bell Pearson, Esq. *right* An early Victorian taperstick. Edward Barnard & Sons. London, 1839.

139

140

facturing firms which subscribed to them. *The Art Journal* itself published designs which were taken up. On the whole, naturalistic detailing is reduced. This we can see from a design, provided by T. Woodington, for a jug decorated with plane-tree leaves, which was copied with only limited success by Gough & Co. of Birmingham.

By the time of the Great Exhibition there was already a move away from the grosser forms of naturalism.

From about 1840 there was a decided return to classical forms. The tradition of copying Roman objects, which Flaxman, Rundell's and Storr had started, was revived, but now on a larger scale due to the improved production techniques. Electrotype facsimiles were produced in large numbers. At Elkington's art advisers and designers such as Sir Benjamin Schlick, a Danish architect, provided moulds which could be repeatedly used. Edward Barnard & Sons also made copies of Roman cups. The cup illustrated was also copied by the pottery firm of Minton, showing how widespread the 'antique' revival was. 'Old Roman' designs and 'quaint forms of the Renaissance' were highly approved of by the critics.

In the late 1840s copies of the Portland Vase were made by Hunt & Roskell, probably from dies once used at Rundell's. The form of this well known piece probably led to the production of the long-necked rounded bodies which were associated with the jugs and coffee pots of the 1850s. The liberty of treatment which one finds in the naturalistic style carried over into the treatment of classical motifs. These had already been freely adapted in the 1820s, but in the 1840s they were revived in a purer form. This was reminiscent more of Adam than of Storr. Bands of engraved key pattern appears, but with beading and gadrooned borders. A tureen in this 'Greek' fashion was displayed by James Dixon & Son at the Great Exhibition. Elkington's, for instance, were to register designs for a whole dinner service in the same style, and by 1860 'Greek' had become all-important.

Chinoiserie was another form of decoration which reappeared in the 1840s. Although this had nothing like the widespread appeal that it had had during the mid 18th century, its existence cannot be ignored. Once again we must turn to Rundell's and Paul Storr. In 1810 the latter had made a bowl and stand in this style, copied from an early 18th-century original. This had been made to simulate lacquerwork by the introduction of panels depicting Oriental scenes with pagodas and cherry-blossom. No doubt productions of this kind stimulated interest among other manufacturers. A pair of silver-gilt tapersticks of 1818 made by William Elliott, for instance, are in the form of standing Chinese mandarins. Later still the style was incorporated into the prevailing Rococo, as a tea caddy of 1827 by R. & S.

Garrard shows. It is clearly based on the Chinese-Rococo taste of the 1740s and 1750s. In the 1840s tea and coffee sets by firms like Barnard's, Hayne & Cater and Angell's featured finials made as miniature Chinamen seated on tea chests. A silver-gilt christening mug of 1845, made by Robert Hennell, is a good example of this Romantic combination of Chinoiserie and Rococoesque scrollwork.

A revival of interest in religion and medieval history led to the popularisation of the Gothic style. A. W. N. Pugin (1812–1852), who had worked for Rundell's, was the leader of this movement which sought to do for architecture and design what Robert Adam had done seventy years before. Though much of his work was concerned with ecclesiastical buildings and furnishings, his designs extended to teapots and domestic utensils. In this he was joined by John Hardman junior, a manufacturer from Birmingham.

Gothic tea sets, like that shown by Elkington's at the Great Exhibition, were faceted or lobed and generally featured Gothicised engraving. Even salt cellars were adaptations of censers. These were surprisingly popular and were imitated by many manufacturers. Pugin himself disliked the popular versions of his work, as we see from his *True Principles of Pointed or Gothic Architecture*. Although Gothic wine flagons by Lambert and Rawlings were exhibited at the Great Exhibition, the Gothic movement was only one feature of a stylistically complex scene. But it was influential enough to lead Gough & Co, Elkington's and Henry Wilkinson & Co. to make silver and electroplate cruets, salt cellars, sweetmeat baskets, mugs, table silver, tea sets and decanter stands with Perpendicular tracery and engraved 'Gothic' decoration. This style was often confused with 'Renaissance' and 'Elizabethan'. The latter was in fact a style that made use of heavy strap-work, flattened scrolls and cartouches. Often found on salvers, inkstands and tea sets, it was popular after 1840. Garrard's and Elkington's successfully adopted it for their display and presentation plate, while Martin, Hall & Co., Barnard's, T., J. & N. Creswick and others used it in their domestic items. Except in modified terms, it quickly went out of fashion after 1852.

The chief exponents of the 'Renaissance' style, which was usually reserved for exhibition or prestige pieces, were Antoine Vechte and his pupil L. Morel-Ladeuil. Other 'Renaissance' silver of the period, though in reality featuring various motifs from the 'Louis Quatorze' style, came from J. V. Morel & Co. At the Great Exhibition this firm showed a 'silver-gilt vase with handle, representing a dragon', and applied with 'a scroll for inscription supported by children'. A similar piece is now in the Victoria and Albert Museum.

Between 1842 and 1845 Owen Jones published his work on the Alhambra palace. This led to a form of

141 An early Victorian seven-light
centrepiece. John Samuel Hunt for Hunt &
Roskell (late Storr & Mortimer). London, 1848.

142 Robert Hennell, 1794–1868.

143 Martin, Hall & Co., working
from about 1855.

144 A group of jewellery and silver-gilt
exhibited by R. & S. Garrard & Co. at the Great
Exhibition, 1851. From *Industrial Arts of the
Nineteenth Century at the Great Exhibition,
1851*.

144

145 A Victorian 'silver-gilt vase with handle, representing a dragon, and a scroll for inscription supported by children.' J. V. Morel & Co. London, 1849. A similar item was shown by the makers at the Great Exhibition, 1851.

146 An early Victorian silver-gilt replica of an antique cup found at Herculaneum. Edward Barnard & Sons. London, 1840. A design also used by Minton's of Stoke-on-Trent for their productions in stoneware. Collection of Henry Walden, Esq.

145

146

147 An early Victorian coffee pot with chased and applied decoration. Probably Benjamin Smith junior. London, 1848. It is probable that the design for this piece was inspired by the Fitz-Cook water-jug [149].

148 A registered design for an ornamental inkstand. Edward Barnard & Sons. London, 21st February 1850.

149 A design for a water-jug, from 'the antique', by Henry Fitz-Cook. *The Art-Union*, 1848. Note the similarity between this proposed design and the Benjamin Smith junior coffee pot [147].

147

148

149

150 'The Fairy Summons'. A design for a hand-bell, by Henry Fitz-Cook. 'A Fairy, . . . seated at the top of a bell-like flower which his weight has set in motion, appears startled by the noise of the petals against the leaves . . . Could the figure be managed in Parian, the contrast between it and the metal dome would be admirable.' *The Art-Union*, 1848.

Barnard & Sons
Angel St. St. Martins le Grand
London

Inkstand.

149   150

engraved decoration which helped to transform the arabesque style based on the studio of Raphael into the Moresque styles in which 'intricacies of strapwork are nicely blended with the partial effect of foliage.'

During the 1830s and early 1840s lotus-leaf decoration derived from Regency 'Egyptian' styles had been used. In 1849 Hunt & Roskell made a large testimonial centrepiece for Sir Moses Montefiore from designs by Sir George Hayter (1792–1871). Also in this style, the piece was supported on four sphinxes. S. H. & D. Gass of Regent Street, London, displayed an 'Egyptian' centrepiece at the Society of Arts in the same year, just as Garrard's had produced facsimiles of Roman cups in the 1840s. Hawksworth, Eyre & Co. of Sheffield exhibited an 'Egyptian' centrepiece at the Great Exhibition.

In 1855 Henry Wilkinson & Co. produced a pair of electroplated winecoolers. Their barrel-shaped bodies were engraved with human-headed bulls and a figure of an Assyrian king between borders of winged bulls and anthemions. This decoration was taken directly from various illustrations in the book by Sir Austen H. Layard (1817–1894) *Nineveh and its Remains*, published in 1849. English plate, as it were, reflected the findings of intrepid travellers and amateur archaeologists in whose journals the mid Victorian public were keenly interested.

Design-conscious societies produced many formulae to capture the elusive ideal, a synthesis of industrial productions and genuine artistic taste. Some advocated wholesale naturalism, others naturalism with moral or educational overtones. Some thought that a reworking of the Greek or Roman designs would bestow original beauty on manufactured goods. Others merely opted for the superficial prettiness of flowers and Rococo effects, thereby giving up the serious question of design. By 1852 it was obvious that if the Great Exhibition had displayed the best the designers could do, then there was something fundamentally wrong with the philosophy of design. Tentative minds groped towards a theory of functionalism, which in a shadowy way had been implicit in the design schemes of Henry Cole.

The history of silver manufacturing from 1820 to 1850 is of immense importance. It was not an age of simple stylistic transition, like that of the Huguenots. Nor was it one of stylistic conformity, like that of Adam. Like a spent star, silverwork was to beam bright and then contract, a signal to the other arts that neither history nor nature could shield man from the revolution, social and scientific, that was coming. In this the early Victorian art critics were right. The question of progress could not be delayed. Soon not only the 'Louis Quatorze' style, but the silver industry, as Elkington's understood it, would be called in question by the Arts and Crafts movement.

151 A Victorian silver-gilt ewer with inlay
decoration in two-colour gold. W. Smith.
Chester, 1879.

1851 and After

The Great Exhibition was 'calculated to advance our
National Taste', so *The Art Journal* wrote in 1851. It
went on: 'It is beautiful appearances we require, not
recondite ideas of Ornamental Art . . . Dramatic, allegoric,
and ornamental art are totally distinct . . . they may be
combined, but one can never be the substitute of another.'

The silverwork on display at the exhibition was
nothing if not a combination of these elements. Moral
allegories and dramatic renderings of the progress of
the British abounded and were considered beautiful.
In the tradition of history painting, the Great Exhibition
celebrated what had been accomplished. In the
decorative arts it clearly put an emphasis on decoration,
rather than on ideas. Silver-designers were encouraged
to believe that new combinations of old decorations
should pass as genuinely novel. For the next thirty
years progress was to be confined almost solely to the
discovery of new techniques which would produce
even richer decoration. The silverworker was intrigued
more with his technical mastery than with the originality
of his designs. The fundamental view that 'ornament
is now as material an interest in a commercial community
as the raw material of manufacturers themselves'
encouraged firms like Garrard's, Hunt & Roskell,
C. F. Hancock, Angell's and Elkington's to elaborate
new designs based on past silverwork.

An essay written on the Great Exhibition as a lesson
in 'Taste' found that 'nine will comprise the whole
number of the great characteristic developments which
have had any influence on European civilisation:
namely – three ancient, the Egyptian, the Greek, and the
Roman; three middle-age, the Byzantine, the Saracenic,
and the Gothic; and three modern, the Renaissance,
Cinquecento, and the Louis Quatorze.' With this in
mind it could add: 'there is nothing new in the Exhibition
in ornamental design.' The conclusion that R. N.
Wornum (1812–1877) was to come to was that 'In
silver-work . . . the inferiority of the English manufacturer to the French is very striking, though, perhaps,
the most beautiful work of this class in the Exhibition is
German.' In his criticism he objects to the taste for
bright silver, to the application of enamels, 'which are
too varied and too strong in colour for such objects'.
He concludes: 'The very vague taste displayed generally
in modern silver-work is the pure result of this

153 The Northumberland Vase. Silver- and gold-mounted Irish bog-oak inset with semi-precious stones. West & Son, Dublin. Drawing published in *The London Journal*. Exhibited at the Dublin Exhibition, 1853. This vase, for which all the component materials were Irish, features 'Hibernia, seated upon a throne, playing the harp, and supported by dolphins. This is emblematical of the naval advantages she has never yet had the good fortune to enjoy.' It cost 500 guineas. The design is based on 'The Bath of Diana', a cabinet piece of gold-mounted agate, enamel and jewels, made in 1704 by Johann Melchior Dinglinger (died 1731) of Dresden.

injudicious hankering after something new, without the justification of a sound study of the old to warrant it.' Nevertheless Wornum believed that a grasp of the principles of classical or Renaissance styles would produce, not copies, 'but a revival of the taste itself'. Silver from 1850 to 1880 was to attempt various such revivals, using every new technique available.

At the Exhibition of 1851 Joseph Mayer of Liverpool exhibited the William Ludlow presentation piece which he had supposedly made in 1846. The pedestal of this piece, which we have already described (page 63), is an almost exact replica of one made by Barnard & Sons in 1848. It is likely, therefore, that Barnard's (manufacturing silversmiths to the trade) were the real makers. Indeed they are known to have supplied Mayer with the 'Anti-Monopoly' waiter which was also at the Great Exhibition. Manufacturers were free to sell the work of others under their own name.

Stylistic continuity between the pre- and post-Exhibition silversmiths was ensured by the evolution of firms themselves. Storr & Co. became Storr & Mortimer. They then became Mortimer & Hunt, who in turn became Hunt & Roskell. The effect of this continuity on production is seen in a tea and coffee set made by Hunt & Roskell in 1869. The design for it had been used by Storr for the Ashburnham dinner service of 1836. Interestingly a border of ovolo motifs, classical urns, leopards, vines, medallions and masks, which appears on a tray made by Storr in 1810, reappears on a salver bearing the mark of Philip Rundell of 1822. It occurs again on a salver by the other royal goldsmiths, Garrard's, in 1832. In the late 1860s it can be seen on a salver made by William Edwards of Melbourne, Australia, but not before it had featured as the girdle on a wine ewer of 1861 by Smith & Nicholson of London. Another example of the persistence of stylistic details is found on a wine ewer of 1876 by Elkington's. The scroll handle which is applied with a modelled reclining female figure and an infant Bacchanal are clearly based on the marble group *Ino and Bacchus* by J. H. Foley (1815–1874), probably done in 1849 and exhibited at the Great Exhibition. Copeland's of Stoke-on-Trent made copies in Parian, while the group was also featured by the printmaker George Baxter (1804–1866) in his print *The Mountain Stream*. In the 1850s and 1860s John Wilmin Figg made the versions of the ewer handle of which the Elkington ones are copies. This shows how popular adapted or copied details were. Relying on earlier work in this way, silversmiths of the 1860s and 1870s were content to reproduce rather than create new designs. Much the same was happening in America. Although, it is true, the Americans were gradually formulating something like their own styles, they continued to be impressed by European prototypes. Their silverwork of the middle of the 19th century displayed yet another interpretation of those antique forms which had fascinated the companies of London and Paris.

The discovery in the 1850s of vast new deposits of silver in America enabled their business to expand and satisfy an ever-increasing demand. Large manufacturing companies sustained art departments much in the same way as had Elkington's of Birmingham. The Gorham Manufacturing Company of Providence, Rhode Island, for instance, employed Thomas Pairpoint as their chief designer during the 1870s. He had come, via Paris, from Lambert & Rawlings of Coventry Street, London. Gorham's, who early recognised the importance of machine-production, have survived to the present day. Later another talented English immigrant, William J. Codman, exploited the popular Art Nouveau market on behalf of the Gorham Manufacturing Company, and produced many romantically inclined items under the trade-name 'Martelé'.

While Gorham's and Tiffany & Co. of New York led the American field during the latter half of the 19th century, there were many other firms. These included Ball, Black & Co. of New York, S. Kirk & Son, founded in 1815 in Baltimore, and Hayden & Whilden of Charleston. While the latter produced during the 1850s and 1860s gigantic dinner services for cotton magnates' mansions, Kirk's made a wide range of domestic items. Some of their tea sets, for instance, are large and boldy chased with a woodland architecture which seems to anticipate the later creations of Walt Disney. Both in splendour and imagination American silver was increasingly close behind the products of Hunt & Roskell of London, Odiot of Paris, or Wagner & Son of Berlin.

The largest exhibitors at the International Exhibition of 1862, held at South Kensington, were Hunt & Roskell. The catalogue emphasised the quality and the workmanship of their products. In general there was a tendency to look back to past successes. For example, Vechte's Titian Vase, shown in 1851, was redisplayed. The exhibition gave plenty of scope to H. H. Armstead (1828–1905), Alfred Brown and others to display their skill in making and lavishly decorating the testimonial and presentation pieces which were then at the height of their popularity. Likewise Elkington's emphasised the technical accomplishments and the material luxury which their exhibits embody. L. Morel-Ladeuil was the star. His table *Sleep* and his salvers on pedestal bases mixed naturalistic details, such as poppies and lion masks, and 16th-century ornament. A. A. Willms's designs showed a renewed interest in classical details in anthemion motifs, simple scrolls and vase-shapes. Naturalistic elements are kept to a minimum although stylised butterflies and masks appear. These features were combined in new proportions, his figures much reduced in size from those which had dominated so

157 A Victorian parcel-gilt tea set in the 'Japanese' style. Elkington & Co. Birmingham, 1875. With a pair of contemporary Worcester porcelain cups and saucers.

158 *centre* A Victorian electroplated condiment set. Struck with the Patent Office Design Registry mark for 1st March 1873. By the 1870s, roller-skating was a craze which had spread to Great Britain, the United States, Austria and Australia. *left and centre-right* A Victorian salt and pepper pot in the form of a cock and hen. E. H. Stockwell. London, 1891. *right* A Victorian toast rack. Hukin & Heath. London, 1897. Similar novelty toast racks were sold at this period by Wilson & Gill, of Regent Street, London, in both silver and electroplate.

157
158

159 A cup and cover with enamelled decoration. Nelson Dawson. London, 1903. Victoria and Albert Museum, London.

160 'Genius'. One of a set of four Victorian table candlesticks, designed by G. A. Carter for Hunt & Roskell (late Storr & Mortimer). London, 1889.

160

161 A pair of Victorian teaspoons with cast and chased handles. Francis Higgins. London, 1857.

many of the candelabra in the 1851 Exhibition.

In the field of electroplate the items displayed showed a great advance. By now Sheffield plate had been almost entirely supplanted. The designs for this were a mixture of past and present ones. The jugs, tea and coffee sets, vases and dessert stands which firms like Derry & Jones of Birmingham exhibited were in the Rococo, Elizabethan or Gothic manner. The latter style was well represented by the work of Hardman's and Hart & Son of Birmingham. A claret jug by John Hardman Powell was 'entirely of hammered work and engraving, no part being machine-stamped'. This was a virtue which was increasingly to be stressed by art critics and silver-craft workers. More than any stylistic novelty or new technique could indicate, the Exhibition of 1862 saw the glimmerings of that concern for 'craft' which marks a revulsion against the endless repetitiveness of styles and their further debasement by machine-production.

In the eleven years between the two Exhibitions every attempt was made by English silver designers to excel their French counterparts. The Exhibition of 1862 disappointingly showed a continued French superiority in the ornamental arts. In the next two decades jewellery and enamelling were to be adopted in an attempt to create richness and originality. By the Paris Exhibition of 1878, however, the impetus which had begun with Rundell's, Paul Storr and Benjamin Smith had exhausted itself. With the exception of Elkington's, who continued to exhibit prestige and display plate, few of the other silver firms which had featured so prominently in 1851 and 1862 now took part. Mostly they were content to mass-produce the vast amounts of popular and useable silver that the domestic market required. It was left to Sampson Mordan & Co., George Unite of Birmingham, Jenner & Knewstub, Messrs Dee, J. B.

Hennell, and E. H. Stockwell to cater for the novelty market. Hennell specialised in good-quality pepperettes, cigar lighters and scent bottles, usually cast in the form of animals. Walter Thornhill of Bond Street produced a range of items suitable for presents, such as match-boxes, scent bottles and pepperettes shaped like tubes of paint. Mordan's, who had started making pencils around 1813, specialised in good-quality pens and propelling pencils. By the 1880s they were producing silver-mounted claret jugs, but are best known for their memorandum and card cases, scent flasks and vinaigrettes, many of them engraved with scenes from the children's books of Kate Greenaway (1846–1901). E. H. Stockwell, a small-worker, was one of the finest makers. A scent bottle in the form of an onion made by him in 1881 is an exquisite production. George Fox, a descendant of Charles Fox of the 1830s, produced a large range of both domestic and novelty items, for example a silver-gilt claret jug in the form of a grotesque bird. The original was a Viennese white porcelain jug of the middle 18th century, which in turn had been adapted from a Mosan (i.e. from the Meuse river region) Romanesque example of about 1160. Charles Stuart Harris, especially in the 1880s and 1890s, made many copies of late 17th-century and early 18th-century English silver. A series of owl-shaped pepperettes of various sizes was made at about this time by E. C. Brown.

The first friction matches were made by John Walker, a druggist of Stockton-on-Tees, who first marketed them in 1827. In 1831 Walker's matches were improved by the Frenchman Charles Sauria. Sauria failed to patent his formula which was then widely used. It produced a disease known as Phossy Jaw among the matchmakers. Added to this hazard was the constant danger of fire. Although the safety match was invented

162 A Victorian silver-gilt casket or tea caddy, 'from the Antique', 'enriched with chased Medallions of Antony and Cleopatra'. Joseph Angell junior. London, 1859. A similar example was exhibited at the Great Exhibition, 1851. Victoria and Albert Museum, London.

 163 George Unite, working from about 1838.

164 James Barclay Hennell, 1828–1899.

 165 George Fox, working about 1860–about 1900.

167 George William Adams of Chawner & Co., mark used from about 1840.

in 1845, Sauria's matches were used for the next ninety years. Silver matchboxes (vesta or fusee boxes) are always fitted with a corrugated striking surface. One of the earliest is a silver-gilt example, made in 1854 by Rawlings and Summers. It is engraved with leafage which on one side frames a chimpanzee. The animal is holding a smouldering bomb! Another, made in 1888, is in the form of a wickerwork basket. Beneath the hinged lid is another lid which is decorated with two embossed and enamelled fishes.

Fuseé boxes, holding a wick of knitted material which was intended to smoulder, were a later improvement of the vesta box or matchbox. They were intended for those who wished to light a cigar or cigarette in a high wind! These often had compartments for flints, matches and a cigarcutter. One, made in the form of an anchor, by H. W. & L. Dee (1872), is of a registered design, and was retailed by Jenner & Knewstub.

Ivory scribbling tablets had been known as 'étuis' during the 18th century. It was not, however, until the early 19th century that memorandum and visiting-card cases became popular. Card cases were particularly common, being small and decorative.

Table silver was, and is, the most popular item of domestic silverware. Knives, forks and spoons are used by everybody. The most prolific makers of the 19th century who specialised in their production were George W. Adams, of Chawner & Co., and Francis Higgins & Son. Both supplied such important firms as Garrard's and Hunt & Roskell, and both exhibited successfully at the Great Exhibition. Apart from his 'Canova' pattern, Adams manufactured more utilitarian wares, such as the 'Tudor', 'Corinthian', 'New' and 'Palm' patterns. Higgins, on the other hand, seems to have specialised in more decorative items, producing finely worked dessert cutlery. This often had handles modelled after 16th-century wood or ivory originals, with cherubs or Bacchanalian figures which had gained popularity ever since the silversmiths Edward C. Farrell and William Eley had started experimenting with more adventurous designs at the beginning of the century.

From 1865 onwards Japanese art had a pervasive influence on both English and American metalwork and design in general. It was applied to interior decoration, furniture and fabrics with striking effect. As Ian Bennett says, 'It illustrated the fact that the finest Victorian designers were capable of absorbing and understanding a new and alien style.'

Much of the Japanese influence stemmed from items shown at the Dublin Exhibition of 1853, and the Exhibition of Japanese Art of 1862, held in London. In 1876 the style was given fresh impetus when firms like Tiffany's in New York and Elkington's in London invited Japanese sword craftsmen, who had been made redundant with the collapse of Japanese military rule,

166 A Victorian 'Louis Quatorze, Style Irrégulier' presentation ewer on stand. Edward Barnard & Sons. London, 1859. Won by the Earl of Howth's *Botheration* at the Howth Races of 1859. Supplied by the manufacturers to West & Son of Dublin for £84 17s. 1d.

168 Francis Higgins & Son, working during the 19th century.

169 William Eley, working from about 1808, died 1841.

to design metalwork. The Anglo-Japanese style that followed, with its use of bright-cutting and bamboo motifs, was easily copied. Outlines were simple, and the engraved scenes were easy to adapt. For example, fish, water-reeds and crabs were commonly applied or engraved on to a simple cylindrical vase-shape.

In spite of Robert Edis's criticism that 'Nothing can be worse than an art at second-hand . . . ', Elkington's and Barnard's produced some interesting Anglo-Japanese articles, including mugs, tea caddies, biscuit boxes, cups and saucers, tea and coffee sets, cutlery and card cases. Some of these items were 'Japanese' only in their areas of bright-cut or engraved formal motifs. Others have the curved-edged cube-shape, decorated with palm-trees, medallions containing storks, and formalised rainbow or fan engravings at the corners.

Tiffany & Co. were the most successful in this field of Japanese exploitation. Founded in 1837 by Charles L. **175** Tiffany, they started as a luxury retail store specialising in fine fabrics, metalwork, jewellery and glass. Their importance grew until, by about 1848, Gustave Herter, a silver designer from Germany, joined their art studio. This liaison did not last, however, and Herter soon left to open a cabinetmaking shop on Mercer Street.

Ever since the beginning, Tiffany's had relied heavily on John C. Moore's manufactory of silverwork. It was not until 1868, however, when J. C. Moore's son Edward became a director of Tiffany's, that the two companies were amalgamated. Although he had worked for Tiffany & Co. exclusively since 1851, Edward C. Moore (1827–1891) now headed their art department. His particular interest lay in Oriental art, and the collection he formed eventually went to the Metropolitan Museum. Like Christopher Dresser in England, Moore was an early devotee of Japanese design. The inspiration engendered by his own collection coloured the designs for his metalwork. These are characterised by an eclectic use of both Oriental and traditional motifs. His ideas appear not as in the clarity of Dresser's work, but more in the manner of A. A. Willms and his employers, Elkington & Co., in England. Whereas Willms's designs remain largely derivative and sentimental, Moore's retain the vigour of inspired reinterpretation. In the words of the Paris dealer and art critic, Samuel Bing, they could be counted as 'original designs in a new style'. Following Moore's direction, Tiffany & Co. rose to be the world's most significant manufacturers of silver in the Japanese style. Display, as well as less prestigious, pieces continued to flow from their workshops, creating an example as well as a national style.

Perhaps the person who grasped the salient strength of Japanese designs more than anyone was Christopher Dresser (1834–1904). Through his abstraction of the principles of Japanese architecture and metalwork, he evolved a functional concept of design which was

170 An American parcel-gilt covered
sugarbowl. Tiffany & Co. New York, about
1875.

171 A Victorian silver-mounted drinking
horn. George Fox. London, 1873.

revolutionary. Japanese influence, therefore, was felt not simply in the form of novel decorative motifs, or even in the new techniques of inlay decoration, but in terms of the adaptations of form and decoration to function.

The best work in this style was done before 1882, the year in which Dresser published *Japan: Its Architecture, Art and Art Manufactures*.

On his visit to Japan in 1876 Dresser gained first-hand experience of Japanese designs. Consequently the work that he did for James Dixon & Son, Elkington & Co., and Hukin & Heath allowed him to apply the structural and functional qualities of Japanese design. Since much of his work is unsigned, it is debatable whether he actually designed the pieces in this style produced by these firms. He is known, however, to have designed a claret jug for Hukin & Heath which shows that the principles of functional simplicity were now being used to produce something new rather than a piece simply in the 'Japanese' style.

Christopher Dresser was probably indebted to the concepts of Henry Cole's circle, and to Owen Jones in particular. The latter propagated his ideas in a series of lectures entitled 'The True and False in the Decorative Arts', given in 1852. Also, the training that Dresser had received at Somerset House School of Design combined with his understanding of organic function which he derived from his botanical training. Flowers develop their forms according to their needs. It was to be a question no longer of using nature as a source of decorative details, but of understanding the functionalism that it embodied. A minimum amount of material was to yield maximum results. Christopher Dresser achieved this in a brilliant way. The teapot illustrated signalled the advent of modern design. It even anticipates the stalwart functional designs of C. R. Mackintosh (1868–1928) which were often devoid of ornament. Its simplicity stands in contrast to the 'Thalia', 'Uxbridge', 'Heraldic', 'Elizabethan', 'Aberdeen', 'Plantagenet' and 'Prince of Wales' pattern tea and coffee sets of Barnard's, Savory's and G. J. Richards. These were 'richly chased' or 'Tastefully Engraved in Wreaths', and on average cost £45. 'Engraved Antique designs' were even more expensive, while the plainest, the 'Cottage' pattern, was considerably cheaper. Such elaborate tea services are described in A. B. Savory's illustrated price catalogue for 1855 as 'of unusual elegance and well-adapted for presentation'.

In his solution of the problem of design, Dresser faced up to the hard fact that machine-production was now a feature of modern life. In this he was unlike William

172 A Victorian parcel-gilt ewer and dish. Elkington & Co. Birmingham, 1874. The dish is one of a pair illustrative of the months of the year, designed by Léonard Morel-Ladeuil.

Morris (1834–1896), and C. R. Ashbee (1863–1942) whose concept of a revived art was a return to the skills of medieval craftsmen. Ashbee's ideal, like Ruskin's, was the craft ideal. The Gothic style had largely died in the 1870s, but it bequeathed the high ideal of craftsmanship to the next generation of designers.

The silver which Ashbee produced was full of finely drawn wires and carefully raised domes. His decoration reflected an appreciation of folk art more than a grasp of functionalism. The delicate tendrils 177 of a decanter made in 1904 by the Guild of Handicrafts, founded by Arthur Dixon (1856–1929) in 1890, and James Powell, suggest Art Nouveau. The chrysoprase finial, however, is more reminiscent of the work of Pugin and William Burges (1827–1881).

The designs produced by Archibald Knox (1864–1933) and Jessie M. King (1875–1949) for Liberty's are in a similar tradition. Their Cymric and Tudric designs reflect the craft spirit and a preoccupation with Celtic art. Archibald Knox's designs are typified by rather simple Celtic motifs and blue or green enamelling. Flowers are stylised into rectangular decorations which occur at the corners of his work, or in rows; sometimes mother-of-pearl was added. To this extent, they built on foundations laid by Joseph Angell and the Italian

metalworker Antonio Cortelazzo (1819–1903), as much as on medieval inspiration.

A designer whose work closely resembles that of Christopher Dresser was C. F. A. Voysey (1857–1941). In appearance it is as utilitarian, if less harsh. The work of Philip Webb (1831–1915) for Edward Burne-Jones and the Arts and Crafts movement has the same functional discipline as Dresser's, but the attention paid to craft details like hammering and burnishing aligns it more with that of Ashbee. The same might be said of the work of W. H. Haseler whose hand-raised silverwork for Liberty's relishes the beauty of a form that is perfectly suited to function. The craft aspect of his work could accommodate Art Nouveau details which in Dresser's work were extraneous. One cannot help feeling, however, that the beauty of Haseler's work depends as much on these details, which are neither essential nor inessential to the design, as it does on functional clarity.

Another designer whose work preserves the individualism of the craft movement while incorporating a sense of functional simplicity was Nelson Dawson (1859–1942). Like Ashbee, Dawson uses cabochon-cut stones and blistered pearls. Decorative details on the covers of cups and other items are often executed in cloisonné enamel, a technique Dawson learned from

173 *left* A Victorian milk jug modelled in the form of an 'Egyptian' harpy. James Barclay Hennell. London, 1877. *right* A Victorian table cigar-lighter modelled in the form of an Indian elephant with mahout. J. B. Hennell. London, 1879.

174 A Victorian teapot, designed by Christopher Dresser for James Dixon & Sons. London, 1880. This is believed to be the only signed piece of silver by Dr Dresser. Collection of Ian Bennett, Esq.

175 An American vase in the 'Japanese' style, with engraved and applied decoration. Tiffany & Co. New York, about 1895.
176 A Victorian rosewater dish, chased with leaping salmon. Gilbert Marks. London, 1899.

173

174 17

177 A silver-mounted green-glass decanter, designed by Charles Robert Ashbee for the Guild of Handicrafts Ltd. London, 1904. Victoria and Albert Museum, London.

178 A covered bowl. Omar Ramsden. London, 1929. The Worshipful Company of Goldsmiths, London.

175

176

178

Alexander Fisher (1864–1936) whose designs required near-virtuoso skill. Ashbee and Fisher were perhaps the artist-craftsmen most admired abroad around 1910. They adapted craft work to 20th-century phenomena in their designs for electric light brackets in aluminium.

178, 180 The work of Omar Ramsden (1873–1939) and Alwyn Carr, who registered their joint mark at the Goldsmiths' Hall in 1898, is also individualistic in this craft sense. Perhaps the identifying feature of their work is the hammer-mark finish. As with the designs of Archibald Knox and Jessie M. King, Ramsden was inspired by Celtic art, though his more important commissions were usually in a Tudric style. His later work is distinctly indebted to the graphic art of Hans Holbein. It was Omar Ramsden, however, who was responsible for popularising the principles of the Arts and Crafts movement by advocating its mass-production, no doubt to the horror of the purist-minded in the craft movement. Until his death he continued to produce individualistic work in a style which hardly altered.

In the 1890s the most popular silver-craftsman was probably Gilbert Marks (1861–1905). His work was praised in the art periodicals of the time. He did not appeal to the folk-designers like Ashbee and Knox. Instead his flange-shaped plates and baluster-shaped beakers were embossed with readily recognisable motifs, like apples, flowers, leaves and, more rarely, fish. This realism was less recherché than complex Celtic patterns, and therefore more acceptable in an age which still found the formalised abstract decorations of Art Nouveau difficult to appreciate.

Henry Wilson (1864–1934) was an architect-turned-craftsman. Succeeding the ecclesiastical designer J. D. Sedding in 1891, he continued his work for church decoration. He designed few domestic articles. His designs favoured polygonal shapes, compact curved lines and rounded bases. To these were added sculpturesque and symbolist elements, much in the tradition of William Burges. He also uses embossed floral patterns, though in a more formal way than Gilbert Marks. His designs were praised in Germany where he received the great gold medal at the 1909 Düsseldorf Exhibition. He was perhaps the only member of the Arts and Crafts movement who confidently modelled the human figure, due to his training as a sculptor and foundryworker. Putti are often found on his work, which also extended to enamelled jewellery.

It was W. A. S. Benson (1854–1924) who more than anyone attempted to reconcile the craft spirit of William Morris, whose firm he took over in 1896, with commercially viable designs in the Christopher Dresser sense. In his Bond Street shop, opened in 1881, and his Hammersmith factory, Benson tried to show that commercialism did not rule out good designs. His jugs and teapots are bold in their efficiency. Specifically

designed for mass-production, they were made in silver, electroplate and other metals. His favourite shape for kettles and teapots was a compressed sphere, with spool-shaped collars and octagonal spouts. The quality of his design was appreciated by the protagonist of Art Nouveau in France, Samuel Bing.

These artists formed a community of craftsmanship in which a common outlook on the art of design in relation to folk patterns and craft traditions did not prevent them from developing their individualistic styles. In this they fulfilled Ashbee's ideal. On the other hand, they treated design with the progressive spirit of Christopher Dresser, though less brilliantly, for their products were less amenable to mass-production except in a debased form. Shapes remain simple and functional though decoration was usually derived from medieval or Celtic art, or indebted to the formalised naturalism of Art Nouveau. In their work, especially that of Nelson Dawson and W. A. S. Benson, construction is emphasised in the honest exposure of rivets and hammered surfaces. Unlike Christopher Dresser, they worked for a limited informed public, neglecting by default the problems that artists who designed for mass-production had to face. To this extent they perpetuated the craft of the individual silversmith rather than the retail manufacturing tradition of Elkington's.

Silver design from 1850, therefore, is complex. It could be called eclectic and be damned by the epithet. It was a period of both perplexity and freedom for the designer who was working in an ancient medium (silver was known in Sumeria in 4000 BC) which now had to face up to the demands that a technological revolution had made. The new techniques gave him an unparalleled ability to do in minutes what had taken Paul de Lamerie months. He cannot be faulted for using this ability. In the silverwork of the 1860s it is clear that a concept of design which had lasted 2,000 years was coming to an end. The mixture of total mastery, technical brilliance and an almost complete lack of a sense of direction suggest that an era was coming to a close. What was a period of technical brilliance was to be superseded by a period of rapid decline in which revolutionary concepts were quietly making their way. It is interesting that the silver of the late 19th century should show such radical change. The germ of the revolution that was to burst with Christopher Dresser had been contained in one aspect of naturalism which stressed the merit of natural function rather than the merit of fine decoration. Silver, if it were not to be a sideline for the wealthy few, had to accommodate the dawning age of aluminium or remain a craft-art largely ignored by a society that found new status symbols in its search for dignity.

Glossary

anthemion
or 'honeysuckle' motif. Inspired from classical architecture, it is found on much silver and **Sheffield plate** of the late 18th and early 19th centuries. Characterised by regular or irregular lobate fronds springing from a common source.

applied work
Details (spouts, handles, etc.) and decoration which have been cast and then soldered on to the object. **Cutcard work** is also applied in this way.

baluster
An elongated pear-shaped form, so called from similarly shaped pillars used to support stair-rails or balustrades. This term, which frequently appears in auction and other catalogues, is convenient for describing the shape of certain hollow-ware (jugs, etc.) or cast items.

beading
Beads, usually cast in rows and then applied to borders of salvers, cruet frames, etc. Especially popular during the last thirty years of the 18th century, and revived a hundred years later.

bright-cut
A popular form of decoration in England, America and Scandinavia about 1770–1800. It is executed with a polished, spatula-shaped tool. Details, such as husks, festoons and flowers, are gouged out, leaving bright clean strokes which are intended to catch the light. (See **engraving**)

Britannia metal
A pewter-like metal otherwise known as white metal. First used by James Vickers of Sheffield about 1769. Later **electroplated** and manufactured in quantity for a cheap market by such firms as James Dixon & Son, Kirby, Smith & Co., and J. Wolstenholme, all of Sheffield. Ingredients varied, but usually consisted of about 448 parts of tin, 20 to 60 parts of antimony, and 5 parts of copper.

Britannia standard silver
Introduced by Act of Parliament in 1697. Compulsory use abolished in 1719. (See page 10)

bullion
Ingots of uncoined gold, silver or other metals produced to a specified standard.

cartouche
A device to contain the owner's initials, crest or armorials, or inscriptions. Usually engraved, but sometimes cast and chased. The engraving of these details reached a peak of excellence during the first three decades of the 18th century. They often formed a major part of the overall design, incorporating masks, shells, leaves, etc., against hatched (brickwork) grounds.

casting
Cast details (handles, spouts, feet, **applied** decoration, etc.) are produced from moulds, and then soldered on separately. Candlesticks, especially of the first half of the 18th century, were manufactured by this method.

chasing
This is a vague term which can be applied to almost all work carried out on the surface of the metal which involves shaping or decoration without the removal of any metal. It is not to be confused with **engraving**. Chasing can be applied to work done on casting to highlight texture or definition, or, as in the case of mid 18th-century domestic items, where flowers, leafage, etc. are worked in low relief into the surface. (See **flat-chasing** and **repoussé**)

Chinoiserie
A term generally given to that type of **flat-chasing** done on English silver about 1675–1685. It was a short-lived fashion inspired by lacquerwork and other imports from the East, characterised by exotic birds and plants, or human figures in rocky gardens.

cleaning
Silver which is in continual use will probably need no more than washing gently in warm soapy water. It should then be rinsed well, and thoroughly dried with a soft cloth or chamois leather. Silver which is very tarnished or black can be treated with several of the proprietary solutions now available. The directions, however, should be *carefully* followed.

cutcard work
This is a form of decoration which was popular from about 1670 until the 1720s. Thin pieces of silver, usually cut into leaf or strapwork patterns, are carefully soldered on to the surface of the piece.

diaperwork
A geometrical or similar pattern often **flat-chased** into silver, particularly about 1735. It is characterised by lines crossing diamond-wise forming lozenges, with the spaces filled with parallel lines, leaves, dots, etc.

electroplate
The technique of coating base-metal objects, usually copper or nickel (see **German silver**), with gold or silver by means of electrolysis. (See page 61)

electrotype
Electrotype copying, akin to **electroplating**, was a technique pioneered by Elkington & Co. of Birmingham. It enabled items to be copied exactly in metal (usually copper or silver) by electro-deposition.

embossing
The raising of decorative details on metal without further texturing. A term sometimes used to describe the rich details of 19th- and 20th-century steam-pressed or rolled silver. (See **repoussé**)

engine-turning
In fashion as a means of decoration about 1810–1860, both in England and abroad. Used on snuffboxes and other small items as area decoration, executed on a lathe and sometimes contained within borders of **engraved** foliage.

engraving
Engraving is a fundamental form of decoration. It involves the incising of a design or inscriptions with sharp-pointed tools which gouge out the metal. **Bright-cut** decoration is a form of engraving. It is quite unlike **chasing**, **flat-chasing**, etc., which do not involve the removal of metal.

fakes
A diverse and complicated subject. The careful collector, however, need not worry if he seeks expert but impartial advice. For English silver in England, the consumer is fully covered by Act of Parliament and the workings of the various Goldsmiths' companies.

feathering
A type of **bright-cut** engraving often used on early George III table silver. Characterised by feather-like strokes along the edges of handles.

flat-chasing
Very low relief surface decoration. None of the metal is actually removed, so it should not be confused with **engraving**. Unlike the latter, flat-chasing leaves a slightly raised impression on the rear of the article so decorated. Much in fashion during the 1730s and 1740s, it was revived during the first half of the 19th century.

fluting
Short or long indented mouldings which are arranged in parallel rows. Especially popular during the late 18th century, when used to great effect by such London silversmiths as John Schofield.

German silver
or nickel silver. An alloy of nickel, copper and zinc. First produced commercially in 1830 by Samuel Roberts of Sheffield. At first it proved too brittle for general use, but with various improvements eventually rivalled copper as the core metal for **Sheffield plate**. German silver was extensively used in the manufacture of **Electroplate**: hence, E.P.G.S. (Electroplated German Silver), and E.P.N.S. (Electroplated Nickel Silver).

matting
Matted decoration was favoured during most of the 17th century. In particular it is found in wide bands on the barrels of tankards and cups, or as surface decoration to salvers, etc. It is a method of texturing the surface by repeated hammer-blows. Also much used as a ground or surround for other decoration (e.g. **flat-chasing**), and in this form survived into the 19th century.

parcel-gilt
Simply an old fashioned term meaning 'partly gilt'.

plate
A collective term used to mean all items of display and domestic silver and silver-gilt articles. Hence 'Racing Plate', etc.

pouncing
or stippled work. Decorative details or initials pricked lightly into the surface of the metal. Especially popular during the second half of the 17th century.

repoussé
Repoussé is a refinement of simple **embossed** decoration. The metal is carefully beaten out from the back into a high relief design. Once the basic shape is formed, other tools are used on the front to heighten texture and detail. In England this style of rich decoration was fashionable during the 17th century, having been inspired by Dutch originals. Wall-sconces, porringers and dishes in particular were decorated in this way, featuring large flowers, animals and cherubs. Repoussé work as a serious art was revived during the 19th century, notably by Antoine Vecht and L. Morel-Ladeuil. The latter's masterpiece in silver and damascened steel, the 'Milton Shield', now in the Victoria and Albert Museum, is a fine example of the art.

ropework
or cable ornament. Often used as an **embossed** or **cast** and **applied** border or girdle decoration on all manner of domestic and display plate.

Sheffield plate
Said to have been invented by Thomas Boulsover (1704–1788), a button-maker of Sheffield, and extensively used as a cheap substitute for silver from about 1760 to about 1850. Copper is mixed with a little zinc and lead, and then cast into blocks. Slightly smaller blocks of **Sterling** silver are then hammered on to the copper base. After various treatments, the fused blocks are rolled into sheets ready for working or stamping.

Sterling standard
Extensively used in England from early times except during the **Britannia standard** period (1697–1719), and in the best of American silver. (See page 10)

wrigglework
A type of **bright-cut** decoration often found on early George III table silver, characterised by serrated incisions at the edges of handles.

Bibliography

Periodicals

The Art Journal
The Art-Union
Illustrated London News
Journal of Design and Manufactures
The London Journal

Magazine Articles

Bennett, Ian, 'First—the Samurai's swordsmiths came West', *Art and Antiques Weekly,* 20th May 1972.

Bury, Shirley, 'Assay Silver at Birmingham', *Country Life,* June 1968.

Bury, Shirley, 'The Lengthening Shadow of Rundell's', parts 1, 2, & 3, *Connoisseur,* 1966.

Culme, J., 'Silver Tea and Coffee Services', *Discovering Antiques,* issue 64.

Hennell, Percy, 'The Hennells Identified', *Connoisseur,* December 1955.

Houston, John, 'Art Workers in Metal', *Discovering Antiques,* issue 80.

Oman, Charles, 'A Problem of Artistic Responsibility', *Apollo,* March 1966.

Ward-Jackson, Peter, 'Some main streams and tributaries in European Ornament, 1500–1750', part 3, *Victoria and Albert Museum Bulletin,* October 1967.

Books

Adam Silver, Victoria and Albert Museum small picture-book no. 35, London, 1953.

Avery, C.L., *Early American Silver,* New York, 1968.

Bing, Samuel, *Artistic America, Tiffany Glass and Art Nouveau,* Cambridge (Mass.), 1971.

Bradbury, Frederick, *A History of Old Sheffield Plate,* Sheffield, 1968 (reprint of the 1912 edition).

Buhler, K.C., *American Silver 1655–1825,* New York, 1972.

Bury, Shirley, *Victorian Electroplate,* London, 1971.

Clayton, Michael, *The Collector's Dictionary of the Silver and Gold of Great Britain and North America,* London, 1971.

Fallon, John P., *The Marks of the London Goldsmiths and Silversmiths (c. 1697–1837),* Newton Abbot, 1972.

Hayward, J.F., *Huguenot Silver in England, 1688–1727,* London, 1959.

Heal, Ambrose, *The London Goldsmiths, 1200–1800,* Newton Abbot, 1972 (reprint of the 1936 edition).

Hughes, Gerald, *Modern Silver,* London, 1967.

Jackson, Sir Charles J., *English Goldsmiths and their Marks,* New York, 1965 (first edition London, 1921).

Knight, F., *Vases and Ornaments etc.,* London, 1833.

London as it is To-day, London, 1851.

Koch, Robert, *Louis C. Tiffany, Rebel in Glass,* New York, 1964.

Layard, Austen H., *Nineveh and its Remains,* in two vols, London, 1849.

Penzer, N.M., *Paul Storr,* London, 1971 (first edition 1954).

Rainwater, Dorothy T., *American Silver Manufacturers,* New York, 1967.

Ramsey, L.G., (editor, with articles by N.M. Penzer, Gerald Taylor and Shirley Bury), *The Connoisseur New Guide to Antique English Silver and Plate,* London, 1962.

Rowe, Robert, *Adam Smith,* London, 1965.

Steingräber, Erich, *Royal Treasures,* London.

Taylor, Gerald, *Silver,* London, 1965.

Thomason, Sir Edward, *Memoirs During Half a Century,* an autobiography in two vols, London, 1845.

Wardle, Patricia, *Victorian Silver and Silver-Plate,* London, 1963.

Catalogues

The Age of Neo-Classicism. A catalogue to the exhibition held at the Royal Academy and the Victoria and Albert Museum, London, September/November 1972.

The Art Journal Illustrated catalogue of The Great Exhibition, 1851.

The Art Journal Illustrated catalogue of the International Exhibition, 1862.

Descriptive Particulars. A catalogue of silver, silver-gilt and enamelled plate exhibited by Joseph Angell junior at the Great Exhibition, 1851.

Handley-Read Collection: Victorian and Edwardian Decorative Art, an exhibition, Royal Academy of Arts, 1972.

Illustrated catalogue of the Collection of Silver, Ashmolean Museum, Oxford.

Illustrated price list, A.B. Savory and Sons, 1855.

19th-Century America: Furniture and other Decorative Arts. A catalogue to the Exhibition held in celebration of the hundredth anniversary of the Metropolitan Museum of Art, 1970.

Official Descriptive and Illustrated Catalogue of the Great Exhibition of the Works of Industry of all Nations, 1851.

Udy, David, *Neo-Classical Works of Art.*

Victorian Church Art. An exhibition, Victoria and Albert Museum, 1971/72.

Warning, J.B., *Masterpieces of Industrial Art and Sculpture at the International Exhibition, 1862.*

Wyatt, Matthew Digby, *Industrial Arts of the Nineteenth Century,* 1851.

Auction Catalogues

Christie, Manson & Woods, London
Sotheby & Co., Bond Street, London
Sotheby's Belgravia, London
Sotheby Parke Bernet, New York

Acknowledgments

The Authors are grateful to a number of people for advice and information, and to others for permission to use photographs and items from their collections. Among these are Mrs Shirley Bury, Assistant Keeper of Metalwork at the Victoria and Albert Museum, who, kindly agreeing to read the manuscript, made a number of valuable suggestions; Sebastian Bell Pearson, Esq.; Ian Bennett, Esq.; H.R. Jessop, Esq.; Michael Parkington, Esq.; Gale Saunders-Davies; and Henry Walden, Esq. We would also like to thank all members of the silver departments at Sotheby & Co., and Sotheby Parke Bernet Inc., and various members of the staff at Sotheby's Belgravia, in particular Tanda Wilson-Clarke and Jeanette Kinch, for their help and patience at all times. In addition, we wish to thank Philippe Garner, Esq., for allowing us access to his extensive library.

The Publishers are grateful to the following for allowing photography of pieces in their possession: H.R. Jessop Ltd, London 45, 119; Sotheby & Co., London 15, 16, 22, 87, 98; Sotheby's Belgravia, London 132, 140, 151, 158, 160. The pieces in the front jacket illustration were made available by Sotheby & Co. and Sotheby's Belgravia.

The Publishers would like to thank the following for providing photographs: British Museum, London 3, 4; Christie, Manson & Woods, London 1, 7, 14, 47, 67; The Colonial Williamsburg Foundation, Williamsburg, Virginia 37; A.C.Cooper for the Hamlyn Group Picture Library 45, 79, 105, 119, 132, 139, 144, 146, 149, 150, 151, 152, 153, 160; Fitzwilliam Museum, Cambridge 56;

The Worshipful Company of Goldsmiths, London 178; Hawkley Studio Associates for the Hamlyn Group Picture Library 15, 16, 22, 24, 51, 63, 64, 87, 88, 98, 138, 140, 145, 158, 159, 162, front and back jacket; Illustrated London News 133; H.R.Jessop Ltd, London 2, 11, 57, 66, 82, 121; Motif Jewellers Ltd, London 179; Museum of Fine Arts, Boston, Massachusetts 46; New-York Historical Society 83; Sotheby Parke Bernet Inc., New York 147; Public Record Office, London (Crown Copyright) 148; Reilly and Constantine for the Hamlyn Group Picture Library 120; Sotheby & Co., London 6, 8, 13, 17, 18, 19, 23, 33, 34, 35, 39, 50, 54, 55, 59, 60, 61, 65, 78, 84, 90, 102, 103, 104, 116, 122, 141, 166, 172, 173, 176; Sotheby's Belgravia, London 5, 99, 106, 157, 161, 170, 171, 174, 175; Victoria and Albert Museum, London 177.

The makers' marks are reproduced from the following books: 9, 10, 20, 25, 26, 27, 28, 29, 30, 31, 32, 36, 40, 41, 42, 43, 44, 48, 49, 52, 53, 58, 68, 69, 71, 74, 75, 76, 77, 85, 86, 89, 92, 95, 96, 97, 100, 101, 118, 123, 131, 154, 156 and 169 from *Marks of London Goldsmiths and Silversmiths, Georgian period,* reproduced by permission of John P. Fallon Esq. and David & Charles Ltd, Newton Abbot; 12, 21, 38, 62, 70, 72, 73, 80, 81, 91, 93, 94, 107, 109, 111, 113, 114, 115, 117, 124, 125, 126, 127, 128, 129, 130, 134, 135, 136, 137, 142, 143, 155, 163, 164, 165 167 and 168 from *English Goldsmiths and their Marks,* reproduced by permission of the Trustees of the late Sir Charles Jackson. 108, 110 and 112 are reproduced by courtesy of the Wine Label Circle and 180 by courtesy of the Worshipful Company of Goldsmiths, London.

Index

The numbers in bold type refer to illustrations